Sustainable Play

For Lily, Willow and Rosa.
My girls. Oh how I love you.

Sustainable Play

60+ crafts and games for an earth-kind home

SYDNEY PIERCEY

greenfinch

CONTENTS

FOREWORD

As I type, all five of my kids are home on school holidays and a tropical storm is currently sending sheets of rain onto our tin roof. Cabin fever has set in and we could not be happier to have a copy of Sydney's new book here to inspire creativity and connection by way of simple, sustainable crafts – crafts you can make easily from recycled materials found around the house, no need for fancy art supplies or materials.

Sustainable Play is not just an inspiring book of simple, do-able children's crafts. While, of course, the crafts are simple in terms of materials and supplies, the book itself is a wonderful reminder of a back-to-basics approach to creative play where the activity itself is just the start of the journey.

From sourcing the cardboard and other materials to transforming them into a new object, the activities call on us to connect with our kids, to ignite their imagination and to create something from nothing. The creative process is an opportunity to spark curiosity; we can explain how an object is made, what features it has and how it functions. It's also an opportunity to inspire new ideas and possibilities and to encourage different ways of self-expression.

At the end of each activity, you'll have a thoughtfully created handmade craft, which becomes a new toy or play object – a toy vacuum or magic wand, a camera or a telescope. Your child can become a doctor or a fairy or a chef! Who needs a store-bought toy kitchen when you can make your own and then continue to add new objects: a kitchen mixer, a food tray, a chef hat. Hours and hours of roleplay are just waiting to be had!

I met Sydney a couple of years ago when she started contributing creative ideas on the Babyccino blog. Over the years, I have enjoyed seeing snippets of Sydney's family life on Instagram, and have taken inspiration from her many creative ideas. There is a no-fuss simplicity to the way she lives that reminds us all what really matters on this parenting journey: taking time to be present with our kids, to connect and engage with them, to have fun with them, and to plant the seeds of curiosity and wonder in their minds and imaginations.

This is a book we will reference time and time again for new ideas and inspiration. And not just for what to do on rainy days when cabin fever has set in, but for a regular reminder to find joy in the everyday.

Courtney Adamo x

INTRODUCTION

The fact that you hold this book in your hands is incredible to me. It has been an amazing experience to create a playbook full of my family's discoveries, memories and imagination. For us, choosing slow play over quick distractions, and creative ideas over plastic toys truly transformed how we spend time together as a family, how we play, connect and do our part in taking care of the planet.

It began as a collection of lists and notes scribbled in the late nights, and early hours of many mornings. I'd had my first baby the year before and was pregnant with my second. Over the moon and excited for the experience of becoming a mother again, I was also mindful of the change in dynamic that this baby would bring. Lily was already a wonderfully inquisitive, talkative and playful toddler. I pictured a tiny, snoozy, utterly-dependent-on-me baby alongside her and would think to myself, 'How will I manage the busyness? The chaos? How will I ensure quality time with both of them, while allowing some calm for me?' I began to give a lot of thought to this new chapter, the aspects of my life and of motherhood I wanted more of and the aspects I could do without.

Up until that point the busyness of my life had propelled me. But now I make the most of the little moments, take my time, celebrate life's simple pleasures and embrace the everyday. And so, I began to spend those pensive, pregnant nights, visualizing what a slower life would look like. I jotted down ideas of things the children and I could do, play and entertain ourselves with, beginning within the sanctuary of our home.

Willow was born at the end of November, the beginning of winter and the cosiest season to be bundled up indoors. Nights as expected were mostly sleepless, and while I fed a tiny Willow, I'd think up craft and play ideas for Lily and I to enjoy the next day. We made toys and invented games, all from things we found around us, things we had at home already. Empty boxes, jars, loo roll tubes, egg cartons, and so on. Before throwing anything out, I'd think – could this not be used again somehow? The magic of creating toys in this way is that the possibilities are endless. A plastic play kitchen (even a very nice one) will always be a plastic play kitchen – but a cardboard box can be transformed and reinvented over and over again, a doll's house, a shopping basket, toy dinosaurs, a space

suit. The list goes on and on! I realized that playing in this way was not only saving us money, it was allowing my children to develop their imagination and creativity. And in the process we were able to look after the planet by reducing, reusing and recycling wherever possible.

When Willow was nine months old, we moved from the bustle of London to rural, sunny, South of France, a long-time dream of ours. Not sure exactly where we would end up, we packed minimally, taking only our favourite toys, books and clothes. Days continue to be spent crafting, all over the house or out in our garden, using things found around us. Transforming everyday household empties, reinventing classic games, experimenting in the garden, and bringing the outside in has brought us closer together. I began sharing our creations online, and in blogs and magazines, and have been so happy to realize that other families are being inspired to do the same, too. To be able to gather our favourite creations into this book has been an absolute joy.

I hope the prompts within these pages bring joy and connection to your family and home, as they have done for us. That you too enjoy discovering the endless possibilities to create and play in the fortress of your space. I hope this puts smiles on the faces of you and your children and brings twinkles to your eyes. And that play becomes more sustainable for you, too.

With love, from our family to yours

Sydney

CREATIVE NOTES

How to use this book

Each chapter focuses on a different room of the house, with creative ideas to play and make in each one. One way to use the book is to choose something to do according to the space you're spending time in. The contents list at the front also details the different crafts and games you'll find within each chapter, and so if you're responding to your little one's requests on particular activities, this will send you in the right direction. There's also the index list at the back, arranged by materials – use this to quickly find inspiration for a particular material you have ready to use.

Your sustainable craft cupboard

The crafts created by my girls and me are all made from everyday empties. We don't need arts and crafts cupboards overflowing with specially bought materials in order to make and create with our kids. Our most favourite inventions have come from an empty box or a couple of loo rolls and some string. Easy, inexpensive and good for the planet.

With three young children, I also find great value in being able to do more with less. For that reason, the necessary 'ingredients' for each of the crafts or games in this book are never more than six. The book uses the same materials time and time again, just in different ways to achieve different outcomes. For each craft I list what is required, but the most common 'store-cupboard essentials' are:

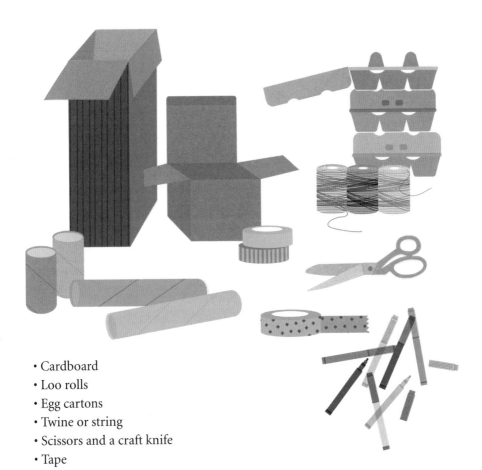

- Cardboard
- Loo rolls
- Egg cartons
- Twine or string
- Scissors and a craft knife
- Tape

I know craft knives may not be a common tool in most homes but they do make a worthwhile investment. However, don't worry if you don't have one, the inner blades of sharp scissors will do the trick just as well.

I don't specifically list colouring pencils or paint in the 'ingredients' lists except for when they are essential. Most of our crafts get left unpainted, or, are decorated later on by the girls as you will see throughout this book. Again, getting messy with paint and colours is not essential for making and creating – unless, of course, you and your kids want to!

Timing and measurements

We've been known to spend all day or all week on a craft, coming back to it over time in quiet moments. Maybe your crafts aren't completed in one sitting either, or maybe they are. Either way, I've intentionally not been prescriptive with how long these crafts will or should take. The timing of them is really to be led by you and your children.

In the same way, when you are putting together your own unique creations, your children will no doubt wish to exercise their own artistic licences! As such, exact measurements aren't proposed in this book, though I sometimes give our measurements as a guideline.

Turning a box inside out

This is how I begin almost every craft. It means any cardboard box can be transformed into anything, irrespective of garish or loud logos! It also makes decorating super simple, providing a blank canvas for the children to make their mark on. You don't need to turn your boxes inside out, but if you'd like to, this is the easiest way I find to do it.

1. Find the seam of the box where the box overlaps itself (usually on an inner corner), which holds it together. If the box doesn't have one, choose any corner.

2. Gently prise this open. I use my fingers when opening up a seam and scissors when cutting along a corner.

3. Now open up the remainder of the box using scissors, if necessary, to cut along any sides that are taped together. You want to turn your box into one flat cardboard sheet.

4. Once you have your flat cardboard sheet, rebuild the box again, with the inner sides (plain, clean cardboard) now becoming the outer sides, and the outer sides (labelled or branded cardboard) now concealed within the box.

5. Finish by taping the box up to secure it, along the seam and any sides previously taped together.

Without further ado, I leave you and your little ones to enjoy your own Sustainable Play.

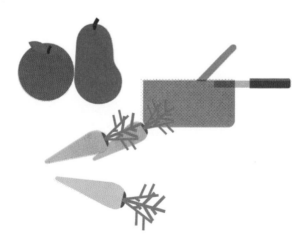

THE KITCHEN

For me, there is no joy to rival that of preparing delicious foods and eating them at a table surrounded by my family. The kitchen is, therefore, a sacred space for me and the rightful starting point of this book. Both my husband and I love cooking and so, from an early age, our children have been in our arms or at our feet while we pottered about in the kitchen. In some ways, the kitchen feels like the 'base camp' of our home. It is here that we routinely return throughout the day. Whether it be for our morning coffee and toast rituals, assembling lunches, putting together the children's dinner or back again to prepare grown-up meals on the nights we eat separately. Not to mention the countless snack and drink preparations in between. I guess the kitchen seems, in a way, to punctuate the day, especially the slow ones, where we drift in and out to graze. As our family has grown, we have explored and enjoyed an abundance of ways to infuse even more magic into this room through craft and connection.

CLEANING IN THE KITCHEN

Doing the chores together was where this book began. I was at home, with two children under two, learning to navigate how to get things done around both of them. It made complete sense to me to get my eldest, Lily, involved with the household jobs. One, because I was grateful for the spare pair of hands, and two, because she was so eager to help. So, I would modify things so that she could do this. We would turn household jobs into opportunities for play and (less intentionally) for learning, too. This would be my first suggestion for an accessible, slow activity to enjoy in your kitchen. Whether your chores list is piled high, or there isn't very much that needs doing (and if this is you, please tell me your secret!), playing at doing the chores is a perfect activity for either.

Washing machine

The cardboard washing machine was the first 'appliance' I made for Lily. I went on to make all manner of appliances, from an iron, toaster and hairdryer, to a record player and a kitchen mixer (see page 41), but this was the very first one. It was a night-time craft, which I did after the kids were in bed, ready for her to wake up to in the morning. While craft is

one of my favourite ways to connect with my children, it's also a great way to connect with myself. I often spend a leisurely evening (while my husband Stuart prepares dinner) crafting something for the girls, or for a friend or for me. I modelled the washing machine on ours and jokingly asserted to Stuart that I'd teach Lily how to put a load of laundry on herself. Unknowingly then, I was right. But it taught me, too, the joy of creating a toy for my child, one she'd go on to use endlessly. It was then that I learned that toys do not have to be store-bought to be brilliant and provide so much fun.

What you will need:
- Large cardboard box
- Small cardboard box
  (or milk/juice carton)
- 2 x loo roll tubes
- Scissors
- Tape
- Optional: bubble wrap
  (for screen), scrap
  paper (for turning dial
  cover), medium-sized
  box (to sit drawer on),
  dinner plate and cereal
  bowl (for outline
  guides), glue

1. **Tape up the front side** of the large box, if it is not taped up already. The back side can be left open to make adjustments from the inside as needed.

2. **Mark out the position** of the detergent drawer at the top, using the small box or carton as a template. Remove the top of the carton, turning it from a box to a drawer. Set the removed cardboard top aside to use for button details later. Cut around the detergent drawer on the large box with a craft knife or scissors, before sliding the smaller box in to place.

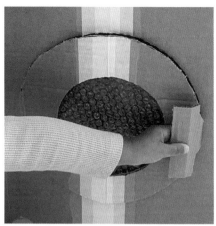

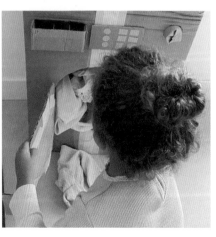

3. **For the machine door,** you'll need to cut out two circles – one for the screen within the door, and the other for the door itself. I used a dinner plate and cereal bowl as a guide for drawing the outlines of these on to the front of the large box. Cut around the cereal bowl outline, removing the cut-out circle completely. Cut around your dinner plate outline too, but only three quarters of the way round to leave a hinge for the door. Fold back the remaining quarter so that the door can be opened and closed (A).

4. **The loo rolls are used as a filter and turning dial** – the filter positioned at the bottom left corner of the machine and the turning dial sits at the top right. Cut around your loo rolls in these positions on the large box to create gaps for the loo rolls to sit in (B).

5. **Before placing the loo rolls in their spaces,** fold the ends inwards so as they appear closed. Alternatively, you can take a circle of scrap paper and tape this across the ends, and your little one can then mark settings onto it. Place your loo roll turning dial and filter into the gaps cut out. To allow your turning dial to actually turn, open the box up from the back side and cut slits all around the end of the roll. Fold these back against the box, and the dial will now turn on the other side.

6. **If you have a medium-size box lying around,** fit this inside your washing machine, so that the detergent drawer sits on top and stays level. Alternatively, you could tape a kitchen roll underneath the drawer (inside the box) for the drawer to sit on.

7. **To finish, add more details if you feel like it.** I stuck a scrap of bubble wrap across the inside of the washing machine door, for a washing bubble screen. I used the set-aside lid of the smaller box to cut buttons out and craft a control panel and an on/off switch.

8. **Tape the back of the box up** when complete!

COLOUR IN THE WASHING MACHINE

This is an idea that came to me one weekend as I was wading through laundry with my keen apprentice by my side. As usual, Lily was so happy helping, busying herself with loading, unloading and passing me pegs. I thought to myself 'How can I engineer it so that she can do this entire sequence independently?' By highlighting the settings I use on the actual washing machine with felt tip she was able to turn the dial to the highlights. Already able to pour the detergents into the drawer, and fill and unpack, this was just the little help she needed to be able to give me the most help! Remember to use a wipeable marker if using pen! I didn't and so my preferred washing highlights still remain on the machine of the first house we rented! Oops. Better yet, colour in little strips of tape or use stickers, so these can be easily removed once they get the hang of it.

Vacuum cleaner

Both my girls are utterly obsessed with the vacuum cleaner, so vacuuming is usually a job I'll give to one of them to do, as it's such a simple but effective way they can help. There were times, however, when they were scared of the vacuum cleaner (Willow) or saw that our dogs were scared of it and so were scared, too (Lily), and this craft would have been great for overcoming that. It also would have been good for the times where they were keen to vacuum, but I was keen for them not to – either because there was nothing to vacuum or I had a headache! But actually, this craft wasn't anything to do with solving a problem, it was just a great way to put to good use a lot of empty kitchen roll tubes we had lying around. Another experiment in my toy making, it worked so well and was so enjoyed by the girls that for a while our actual vacuum cleaner was utterly forgotten and that chore again fell to me!

What you will need:
- Wrapping paper tube (or 3 kitchen rolls)
- 2 x cardboard sheets
- Cardboard box
- Twine or string
- Scissors
- Tape

1. **Begin by cutting the wrapping paper** tube to size. If using kitchen rolls, I found three of these worked well. Tape these together.

2. **Take one cardboard sheet** and cut it into rectangular segments. Make a little stack of these segments, all the same size, for the head of your hoover. Depending on the size of your cardboard sheet you may be able to get lots of the same sized segments, which you can tape one on top of the other, or perhaps you will just have two. Either way works perfectly well. Once taped together, set aside.

3. **Cut four slits in the north, east, south and west** positions at one end of the kitchen roll or wrapping paper tube, and fold these back towards the tube.

4. **Tape these down onto the hoover** head of stacked segments and the stick of your hoover is complete.

5. **Next, turn to the cardboard box,** which is the second part of your hoover. If the box has a lid, you need not do anything. If it doesn't, cut an opening so that the inside can be checked on easily. This box opening represents the home of the dust bag (A). I like to add a few 'real' features to my toys to incorporate some learning and understanding of how the non-cardboard appliance actually works. This might be something your little one wants to draw in or decorate themselves – we stuck in some paper packaging to represent this.

6. **From the second cardboard sheet,** cut two circles for wheels, and two little squares for hoover switch details. We stuck down two switches to the hoover head to represent the switches for carpet or smooth flooring, and used tape on the circle shapes for wheel spokes. Again, your little one may like to draw these on themselves instead. Stick all your details down.

7. **The final step is just to connect the two parts of the hoover.** Cut a long length of twine or string, tape one end to the top of the 'hoover stick' and the other end to the underside of the 'hoover box'.

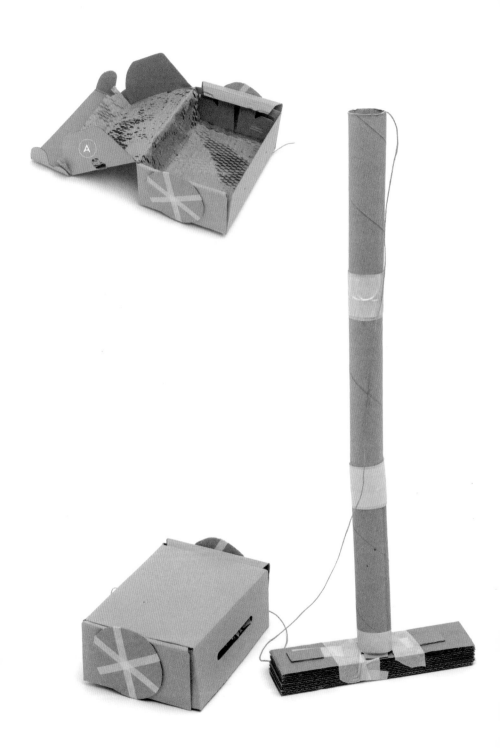

Dustpan and brush

This is a not a creation that Lily instantly took to. She was more interested in the scraps and cuttings made while creating it than the finished article! So, I left it on the coffee table and we went about our day. Later on, I found her emphatically sweeping the kitchen floor (and then the walls) with her new toy! I'm really happy that she enjoys this version, rather than our actual dustpan and brush, which lives under the kitchen sink, dusty and covered in cobwebs! You may choose to begin this craft by turning your box inside out. I always do, preferring to have a plain outer side that my girls may or may not choose to decorate. It can sometimes be tricky to paint over cereal boxes as their often shiny outer layer can require lots of paint (and lots of patience) to entirely cover. If you also prefer a plainer side, see page 15 in the Creative Notes section for my tips on turning your box inside out.

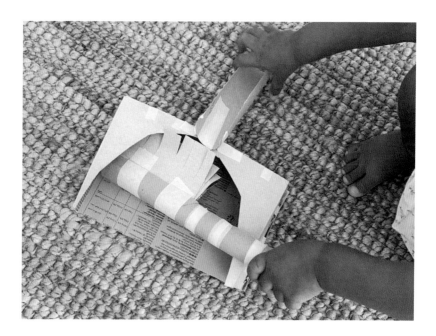

What you will need:
- Cereal box
- 2 x kitchen roll tubes
- Scissors
- Tape

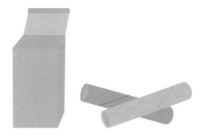

1. **Cut off the top third of the cereal box** and set aside (this will be used for making the dustpan brush).

2. **Take the remaining segment of the box,** cut a semi-circle out of the top face, making sure to leave enough space along the bottom to attach a handle. This will be your dustpan.

3. **Take the set-aside third of the box** and cut this open so you have one long strip. Cut slits all the way along the strip. This can be done by your little one; it's the sort of job that Lily enjoys doing.

4. **Fold the long strip up so it is the same length** as your dustpan. Secure with tape. Push your strips outwards in each direction to further create the bristles on the brush (A).

5. **Now you need to add handles to both the dustpan and brush.** Kitchen rolls make perfect handles for little hands. Take both tubes and cut them open vertically. If your little one enjoys the snipping and cutting aspect of this craft then this is another job for them.

6. **Roll one cut-open tube** back into a tube for the brush handle (B) but make it smaller and tighter, taping it at the base to secure. You can slot your brush into the top of the rolled tube and tape that into place. Your brush is now ready.

7. **Take the other cut-open kitchen roll** and cut it in half vertically to make the dustpan handle (C). Take one half and roll it up in the palm of your hand, as if trying to roll back into a tube, to curve it. Tape this to the dustpan in the centre of the space you left when cutting your semi-circle. Once taped down, the brush handle should slot nicely into the dustpan handle.

FOOD PREPARATION

A lot of my cardboard kitchen creations were crafted to encourage Lily's glorious independence. She's always wanted to do things herself, preferring to dress herself rather than be dressed, feed herself rather than be fed and so on. Giving her the space to do these things has not only been great for her growth, but also great for our relationship. I would often make mental or handwritten notes of things I could leave 'For Lily to do' mindful of the pride and satisfaction it brought her, as well as the important sense of inclusion. When Lily was younger, and on the days I would want to spend an entire morning or afternoon on just one thing, I would prepare recipe ingredients in separate individual bowls for her. Ingredients for a cake for example, all pre-measured, so she could put it all together in sequence herself. While the washing-up pile at the end was huge, it was utterly worth it to see how happy she'd be to have made an entire cake herself. Plus, she was quite happy to get stuck into the washing up afterwards, too.

'For Lily to do':
* Juicing oranges for freshly squeezed juice.
* Grating ginger for juices or cheese for pasta.
* Pouring pre-measured bowls of pancake ingredients into the blender.
* Peeling and chopping bananas for smoothies or cake.
* Sieving flour for cakes.
* Washing vegetables.
* Cracking eggs for cakes or breakfast (and more recently practising separating them).

 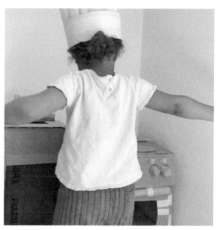

COOKING IN THE KITCHEN

Not only are we big food lovers in our family, we also really enjoy cooking. While my speciality is baking and my husband is great at main meals, the girls are happy to assist us with both. Pulling up a chair to the counter to stand beside us, they flick switches on the kitchen equipment, stir bowls and rinse dishes. The crafts in this section have allowed for all these things, and more, to be practised safely. In this way, the girls can get stuck into cooking whenever they want, either alongside us, or independently in their cardboard kitchen.

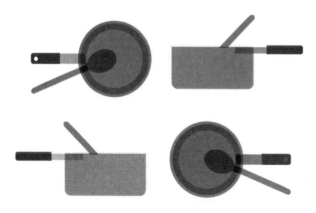

Sink and cupboard

One of the many benefits of cardboard toys is children learning to play gently, taking care of their belongings. It is, of course, totally natural for our little ones to play vigorously at times, especially in their younger years while learning and discovering. Another benefit is that children can witness the time, effort and clever construction that goes into creating

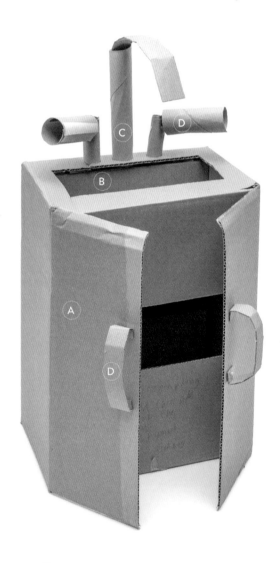

things and, of course, the wonder of re-use. I made this set twice. Lily loved playing with it so enthusiastically that the first one didn't last too long. Making it the second time, Lily pottered around me as I crafted, watching me put the various elements together and understanding the need to be gentler with them. The second version is still going strong.

What you will need:
- 2 x cardboard boxes (1 large rectangular and 1 smaller)
- Cardboard sheet
- 1 x kitchen roll tube
- 4 x loo roll tubes
- Scissors (and a craft knife, if you have one)
- Tape
- Optional: drinking glass

1. **Begin by creating the cupboard.** This is done simply, either by using the cardboard flaps your box already has as doors, or cutting the front face in half and open to make doors (A).

2. **Now to add the sink.** The smaller box will be your sink basin, with an opening for this from your larger box. Remove the top of your smaller box, if it has one. Slot this smaller box inside the larger box, with the open side at the top and tape in place from the inside.

3. **On the top side of the larger box,** cut an opening into the smaller box (B) using your craft knife (or the blade of your scissors). You want this opening to be smaller than the box below so as to leave enough space for your spout and tap handles around the edge.

4. **Once you have the basin** – hooray! – it's time to make the spout and tap handle holes. Take two of the loo rolls and cut these open vertically. Roll them into slimmer tubes and tape back into place.

5. **Do the same with the kitchen roll.** The kitchen roll is for the spout (C) and the loo rolls for the tap handles (D). I placed the kitchen roll spout in between the two tap handles to mirror our sink, you may choose to mirror your own if it is different.

6. **Once you are happy with your chosen places,** use the rolls as a guide and cut out holes into the cardboard box around them.

7. **Cut two strips of cardboard** from the scrap cardboard sheet, no wider than the rolled toilet roll tubes. Pop these inside the tubes.

8. **Take the other two loo rolls** and repeat step 4. Feed these onto the cardboard strips and fold the strip where the rolls meet. You can fold any excess back into the tube so it stays in place snugly. Now the tap handles can be turned on and off by turning the loo roll handles back and forth.

9. **For the spout, cut a thicker strip of cardboard** and slide it into the kitchen roll hole. You may need to fold it at the base so it fits in. For the bit that remains outside of the tube, curve this in your hands to create the spout shape.

10. **The final thing the cupboard needs is door handles.** Cut two thick strips from the cardboard sheet. You can wrap these around a glass to curve them before taping the ends into place on the doors (D).

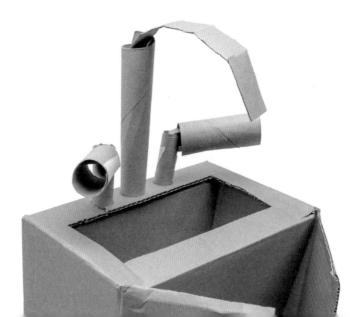

Chef hat

An essential accessory for any budding chef, this is a creation to make and keep on top of the fridge or in a dry spot on your countertop for when your children want to play sous-chef. I love watching Lily potter about the kitchen in this, intermittently shouting 'yes, chef!'

What you will need:
- Cardboard sheet (or paper, for a more delicate hat)
- Tissue paper (baking paper or newspaper work well too)
- Scissors (and craft knife, if you have one)
- Glue
- Optional: ruler, twine and tape or a hair bobble

1. **Cut two lengths from the cardboard** sheet about the width of your hand. I get my lengths nice and straight by using a craft knife and cutting against the spine of a hardback book (I can never locate my ruler). These strips of cardboard will be the headband for your chef's hat. You could use paper for this, but for Lily's magnificent mass of curls, cardboard makes for a far more durable and stable hat.

2. **Place the cardboard strips together** in a line with a slight overlap. Glue or tape these together to create one long length. Again, I use tape for durability. This could now be painted or decorated should your sous-chef wish.

3. **Next, take the tissue paper** (perhaps found rolled up in a box from the inside of a pair of shoes, or set aside from a recent delivery) and cut a rectangle. You want it to be pretty long – longer than the length of your headband and pretty tall, too (the height of two or three of your hands) and for this reason, I used baking paper as it's a little more sturdy.

4. **Make folds in the paper** all the way along and secure them with glue. Glue or tape this to the inside of the headband.

5. **Fit the headband** to the size of your little one's head. Tape or glue the headband ends together to secure the hat.

6. **Now, we create the closed top** to complete your chef hat. Gather together the tops of the hat with one hand, and push this inside the hat, gently pulling it down with the other hand from the inside.

7. **Secure the inside** by tying up the cluster that is the top of hat, with twine, tape or even a little hair bobble.

COOK TOGETHER

Choose a recipe, either from a book, your memory or imagination, and make this with your little one. Prepare the different ingredients together, allowing them to join you but also watch you. Pop them in their high chair if they're really young, or have them stand at the countertop on a chair or a stool, so that they can really be involved. I include some ideas on page 31 for assistance that children can offer. This is one of my favourite ways to spend time in the kitchen with Lily, who is always eager to help. Even just allowing her to do all the stirring, smelling and tasting is welcome participation. Some of our favourite things to make together are: smoothies, vegan banana pancakes, homemade pizzas, summer salads, vegetable soups and a really good tomato sauce.

EGG (OR ANYTHING) AND SPOON RACE

A childhood sports day favourite, the egg and spoon race is a classic. We reinvent it by hunting for a few obscure things that are trickier but no less fun to balance (avocado stone, wooden pegs, colouring pencils). Then we set out a race track. Collect your balancing items together and then set up races with them. You can race your little one or cheer them as they race against themselves. This is also a fun one to set up for siblings or playdates. For older children, you could add in obstacles to make it trickier. Chairs they have to climb up and over, for example, or have them hopscotch through the course!

Kitchen mixer

Just before we moved to France, I began writing for a parenting blog. It was a blog I'd read and enjoyed for such a long time and was so happy to contribute to, sharing my, and the girls', cardboard crafts. This went on to kickstart my contribution to other wonderful blogs and publications and I was delighted to be commissioned by a French parenting blog just after our move, to share a 'never-before-seen' craft and how-to. After much deliberation, and Stuart's suggestion, I decided to create and share a how-to for a kitchen mixer. An actual kitchen mixer had been a

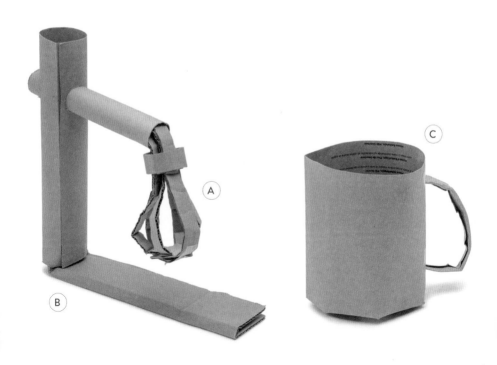

Christmas present from Stuart to me the year before and as a family we had used it non-stop since I opened it. We left it behind on our move and it was missed a lot. So creating a cardboard version was not only about the commission, but also about crafting a reminder of a treasured object. You can use play foods in your mixer if you have them, or cut out little cardboard foodstuffs, which your child can be decorating while you're putting the mixer together.

What you will need:
- 4 x cardboard sheets (2 thin, such as cereal boxes and 2 thick, such as cardboard boxes)
- 1 x kitchen roll tube
- Scissors (and craft knife, if you have one)
- Tape
- Drinking glass

FOR THE WHISK (A)

1. **Cut one thick cardboard sheet** into seven strips. Overlap six of the strips and position in the shape of an asterisk. Tape them in place in the middle.

2. **Wrap each strip around the drinking glass,** pulling it towards you, to give them a curved shape. Then gather the top of the strips together and secure near the end using the remaining cardboard strip and tape in place.

3. **Tuck the off-hangs into one end of the kitchen roll tube,** securing with more tape if needed.

FOR THE MIXER STAND (B)

4. **Wrap one thin sheet of cardboard** around the drinking glass to achieve a cylindrical shape and secure with tape.

5. **Your kitchen roll whisk tube needs to poke** through this so, using a craft knife or the blade of your scissors, cut a hole through each side of the stand for the roll to slot through.

6. **For the base of the stand,** take the final thick sheet of cardboard and fold in half width ways. Fold or squeeze one end of the sheet so that it can be tucked into the bottom of the other piece of your mixer stand. Tape into place if needed.

7. **Now fold the cardboard** to create the flat base of the mixer stand.

FOR THE MIXING BOWL (C)

8. **Take the second thin piece of cardboard,** cut off the top quarter of the cardboard and set aside for the handle. Wrap the remainder around the drinking glass to curve it. Loosen this cylinder shape as you want this to be a lot wider. Secure with tape.

9. **At the bottom of the cylindrical shape,** make six evenly spaced vertical cuts, to about a quarter of the way up. Fold these inwards to create the base of your bowl.

10. **Place a scrap piece of cardboard** over the bottom of this and secure with tape on the inside (and outside if necessary).

11. **Take the quarter you previously set aside** and fold in half lengthways. Wrap this around the drinking glass to achieve a round handle. Cut two horizontal slits into the side of the mixing bowl to feed the handle through at both ends. Secure with tape on the inside of the bowl.

FOOD PLAY

'Don't play with your food' is a common instruction bestowed upon children. However, I'm a big believer that play can be found and enjoyed beyond the realm of conventional toys or a designated corner, just by using your imagination. Play can also encourage fondness towards things our children may at times be ambivalent about, such as mealtimes, having a bath or even life changes, such as moving home or starting school. So, most of the time and in most scenarios, play is encouraged in our house.

For me, the use of food for play (rainbow rice, sensory spaghetti and so on) is conflicting. It can seem lavish and wasteful, something my grandmother would definitely raise an eyebrow to. Using food scraps is, therefore, my preferred approach to incorporating food into play. Odds and ends that would otherwise be composted can be used first as stamps for printing, or food past its sell-by date can be used in sensory boxes – though I am very much working on addressing spoiled foods in our house! With anything new, I will use measured amounts – a cupful of something rather than a whole bag. I hope my doing so models to the girls the importance of being mindful of how we use and consume.

Oven

The oven is such a simple yet effective creation. The use of a sturdy cardboard box means that this is a craft with longevity. Back in London we had a beautiful, heirloom play kitchen that we invested in for both girls. When we moved, I promised Lily that I would find a suitable box and begin making her a new kitchen. I crafted the oven really simply and it lasted us months, played with most days, without needing much in the way of repair. When we moved from our first house in France to our second, which was just under an hour's drive away, we had to make an extra trip just to transport the oven in the back of the car!

What you will need:
- Large cardboard box
- 1 x loo roll tubes
- Cardboard sheet
- Scissors (and craft knife, if you have one)
- Tape
- Glue
- Optional: another cardboard sheet (for an oven shelf and door handle), clear film or tissue paper (for screen), scrap paper (for oven dials)

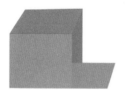

1. **Create the oven door.** Cut an upside-down cat flap opening on the front face of the box and fold this outwards to create a door that can open and close.

2. **Cut a smaller section** out of this first door to create a window to see through and observe food cooking. You could tape a sheet of clear film or tissue paper in place for the screen – we left ours open though.

3. **Now for the oven dials.** Take your loo roll tube and cut it in half horizontally, then cut those pieces in half vertically. Roll them back together tightly and tape into place so you have two slim tubes.

4. **Position these at a good distance** above your oven door and using them as a guide, cut same-sized holes in your oven with a craft knife or scissors. Slot the tubes into these holes and then, opening your box back up so you can reach them from the inside, cut slits in the tubes from the inside of the box and fold them back. This secures them in place while allowing you to turn the dials on the other side.

5. **You can cover the front of the dials** with circles of scrap paper if you wish, and your child can mark settings on them, too.

6. **Next cut four circles out of the cardboard sheet** for the hob rings on top of the oven. Cut squares and buttons for dials as desired.

I mostly mimic our own appliances when making our cardboard versions; you can copy features or buttons from yours. Stick these down with glue.

7. **An optional addition to the oven** is a raised shelf. As you currently have it, the oven door is opened and pots and pans placed on the floor of the box, but you can tape another cardboard sheet inside to create a raised shelf in the middle of the oven.

8. **You could also add an oven door handle.** You can use the same method for this as with the sink and cupboard (see page 34), placing it horizontally at the top of the oven door.

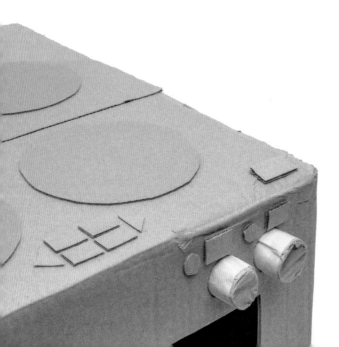

SMILEY FACE FOOD

I often add smiley faces to the girls' food to put a smile on their faces and mine. As they've grown older, we've enjoyed assembling smiley faces together. I cut out shapes and features for them to put together funny faces themselves. I find the meals that work best are mini pizzas, omelettes and open sandwiches. It's also a wonderful way to incorporate less favoured vegetables into mealtimes. We have since moved on from smiley face food to creating pictures with food. Egg and soldiers arranged like a sun is one example we love but really there are endless possibilities!

KEEPING TIME WITH THE OVEN

We love 'keeping time' in our house. We use it as an incentive to get jobs done as quickly as we can (but usually just end up running around in fits of giggles). This is super simple! Decide what job you are going to do, for example unloading the dishwasher or laying the table, then set the timer and see if you can beat the clock. We find this so hilarious as the minute the clock is set, we become giddy and run around like headless chickens getting nothing done! It goes without saying, but I'll say it anyway, to take care when running and playing in the kitchen! My girls know it's not a game that can be played if there's anything cooking on the hob or in the oven at the time.

Breakfast tray

For those of you who have ever had your children look in your kitchen cupboards and ask for the most inappropriate or bizarre thing for breakfast, this is for you. Or rather, this is for them! Be it the chocolate biscuit that you keep for afternoon treats, the slice of cake from yesterday's dessert or just a bizarre concoction that they've conjured in their minds – with this craft they can design and enjoy the exact breakfast tray of their choosing.

What you will need:
- Shoe box lid (or cereal box)
- Cardboard sheet
- Scissors (and craft knife, if you have one)
- Optional: another cardboard sheet, drinking glass, tape (for mug or glass)

1. **Cut out two handles on opposite sides** of the shoe box lid to create a breakfast tray. If you're using a cereal box, cut off the front face to create a tray, and then cut out the two handles.

2. **Use the cardboard sheet** to cut out a circle for a plate and shapes for any other desired breakfast foods. Bread is an easy one and eggs, too. Cutting the silhouettes of shapes allows your child to add their own detailed designs.

3. **Cut out some shapes** for cutlery.

4. **You can easily craft a glass or mug** by rolling a small cardboard sheet around a drinking glass and taping in place. Cut four slits at the bottom and fold inwards to create a base. Add a cardboard strip handle to create a mug.

THE ART OF FOOD

The activities in this section put food ends and leftovers to great use. Great for little ones who enjoy messy play, they also allow for dexterity and co-ordination to be practised in a fun and creative way.

Vegetable printing

This craft is a great way to reinforce the wonders of vegetables! Transform food ends into stamps for pattern and printmaking. Sometimes I carve shapes out of potatoes that are past their best, but the joy of using a variety of vegetables is that they all create and make their own unique shapes. We do this on big rolls of brown paper and later use our prints for homemade wrapping paper.

What you will need:
- Vegetable scraps (potatoes, carrots, end of corn, celery, citrus fruits)
- Paint
- Paper

1. **Once you've carved or cut** your vegetables, the children can unleash their creativity, dipping into the paint and stamping patterns onto the paper.

Tea or coffee painting

This painting play is super quick to set up and can be enjoyed by all ages. I strap Willow into her highchair and tape a scrap of paper to the table part for her to paint on and set Lily up at the kitchen table next to her. Sometimes I sort out dinner while they're painting, other times I join in with them. The paints are made with 'powders', either a scoop of instant coffee, for older ones who aren't going to experiment with putting the paints in their mouths, or hot chocolate powder, for younger ones who might experiment! I use a little espresso cup or an empty egg carton to house the powders. Even just a spoonful of powder on a children's plate would do.

What you will need
- Coffee, tea or hot chocolate powder
- Pot or plate
- Paintbrush
- Water
- Paper
- Optional: pipette

1. **To mix the paint,** take a spoon of powder and add a drop at a time of water until you've reached your desired consistency. Your little one can do this with a pipette, if you have one.

2. **Alternatively, dip a wet** paintbrush into a decanted pot of powder. You can chop and change between these techniques to experiment with lighter and darker shades.

3. **You could also experiment** with spices. Paprika and turmeric work really well with this and it's also a wonderful way to incorporate conversations about senses and smell.

Sensory activity box

When I first came across sensory boxes, I thought of them as something that created a lot of mess and also encouraged a lot of waste. One day during a cupboard clear-out, I found the dregs of a bag of lentils, past their best, and decided to set up a little sensory box for the girls. I was so surprised by how engaged with it they were and it didn't need a lot of lentils like I'd often see pictured. Of course, whatever is used can be kept in an airtight container and re-used again and again. Discovering this mode of play for Lily when she was around two was perfect – she was very aware of what should and should not go in her mouth. It was something Willow was still learning when she started and this meant she needed much more supervision from me. Please remember to be mindful of choking hazards.

What you will need:
- Sensory grains (rice, dry beans, birdseed, peas)
- Cardboard box or container
- Variety of kitchen utensils for scoops

1. **Fill a cardboard box or** container with a measured amount of grains (I usually set aside dregs for this, or if ever I miss a sell-by date, I'll keep for a sensory box).

2. **Tape the box to the table** to dissuade your little one from turning the whole thing upside down!

3. **Offer a variety of everyday items** to use with the box: big wooden spoons, teaspoons, measuring spoons, an egg cup and so on. Loo roll tubes can be used as scoops, if you cut a little spout out of them.

THE JOY OF THE SUPERMARKET

I've always loved food shopping. As a young girl I would know which corner shops had ingredients that you'd never find in the giant supermarket. On summer holidays I'd always be drawn to the markets where you could hand-pick your own fruits, vegetables and spices. When my husband and I first got together, he would come over to my house, open up my fridge and despair. Despite my love of food shopping, my own fridge and cupboards were often bare in those days – I didn't really see the point in doing a big food shop as I would mostly eat out with friends or whip up two-minute noodles for dinner. So, we both love the fact that these days the fridge is full of favourites and of leftovers, of fresh fruit and various veggies and, of course, a bottle or two of wine! Food shopping now isn't just about surveying all the wonderful things, it's about bringing them home and feeding my incredible family.

SUPERMARKET SWEEP

Supermarket sweep is a speedy game to set up and it's great for memory and learning, too, giving your little one the opportunity to practise naming fruits, foods or whatever household items you choose to use. Collect various items from around the house (this can be anything – we've included remote controls, Daddy's slippers and a water beaker in our 'aisles' before) and lay them out along your aisle. We tend to use our kitchen table as the aisle. Once you've identified all the items with your child, it's time to shop! Lily and I take turns in being the shopper and the shopkeeper. The shopkeeper collects and bags up everything the shopper asks for, asks how they would like to pay and remembers to say, 'have a nice day!' We also throw in curveballs such as asking for items that aren't on the table so that the shopkeeper has to apologize and explain why it is not available!

Cash register and scanner

Quickly and simply transform a pair of boxes into an ultimate 'shop play' accessory. The little drawer and receipt details here are my favourite. Simple touches, but they allow for such intricate play. We play with real coins now, but for younger ones, play safe and cut cardboard coins or scrap paper notes to pop inside your till.

What you will need:
- 2 x small boxes (one bigger than the other)
- Cardboard sheet
- 2 x loo roll tubes
- Scissors
- Tape
- Optional: scrap of paper, coins

1. **Begin by cutting out one side of the bigger box** to make an opening. Remove the top side of the smaller box and place it inside the larger one. The small box is your money tray that you slide back and forth for cash and coins (A). You could cut a little thumbhole from this as a sweet detail to help with ease of access to the money drawer.

2. **Cut nine squares from the cardboard sheet** for the cash register buttons (B). Stick these on the register in rows and columns of three. Be sure to leave space above the buttons for the receipt detail.

3. **Tape or glue one of the loo roll tubes** to the space above your buttons (C). A scrap of paper can be rolled around this for a receipt.

4. **Cut a scanner shape** from the cardboard sheet, ensuring it has a long stem.

5. **Take the other loo roll tube** and cut it in half vertically. Place the stem of the scanner inside the cut open tube and then roll it back together tightly and tape to secure (D).

6. **Cut a thin strip of cardboard** and roll it around your finger to give it a round shape. Tape together in a loop. Tape the loop to the side of the box and slot the scanner in here.

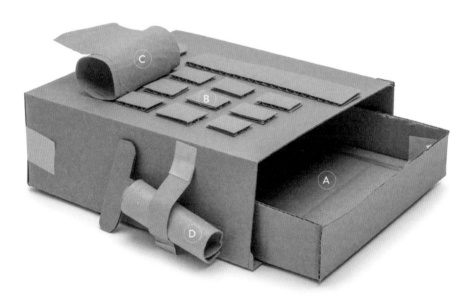

SEASONAL FRUIT AND VEG

I was once asked to give an example of one of the ways having children had changed me. Of the numerous ways, one of the first things that came to mind was my renewed gratitude for the simple pleasures in life. One of these is the changing of seasons – crunchy autumn leaves and pumpkin picking, short winter days followed by blossom in the spring, strawberries in the summertime, clementines at Christmas, and so on. Moving to a rural part of France compelled us to embrace seasonal eating. Local markets and supermarkets offer only what is in season – a total contrast to the year round offerings of mainstream stores back in London. This idea is inspired by, celebrates and explores seasonal produce.

All you need are a handful of materials – a scrap of paper, colouring pencils or crayons and possibly some scissors, glue and cardboard for mounting. Draw seasonal fruits or vegetables for your child to identify or colour. Older ones can take the lead on this themselves. You could keep your sheet of paper as is or cut the pictures out and mount them onto a sheet of cardboard with glue. Put your finished print somewhere, perhaps pinned to the fridge, or the inside of a kitchen cupboard at easy reach for your child. Use it as a reference for mealtimes or recipe ideas and compare your drawings from season to season to see how it changes.

THE LIVING ROOM

True to its name, there's so much living, being and connecting that goes on in this space. So much so, in fact, that I'm not sure which is more of 'the hub' of our home – the kitchen or the living room. Our galley kitchen in London would be filled with kids, adults and dogs, as we cooked and cleaned. Music would murmur away and conversation, too. Yet, once the meal preparation was done, it was our living room where we sprawled out, ready to read, play games or dance.

GAMES AND SPORTS

I love board games. They remind me of cosying up in front of a fire after persuading my husband to play Monopoly or Scrabble with me though he despises both! Until my children are old enough to take over the 'board games with Mum' baton, we enjoy some of the following games and activities as a family. All are very creative, and all are very fun.

Marble run

There's nothing complicated about this one – a sequence of loo roll tubes taped at angles to a wall through which to drop a stone or marble. It's such a joy bringer. We extend the play here with the girls decorating the loo roll tubes beforehand. Once decorated, we build the run together.

What you will need
- Masking tape
- Loo roll tubes and kitchen roll tubes (the more you have, the longer and more complex your run can be)
- Little bowl or egg carton
- Small stone or marble (or bottle cork, any small round object will do)
- Optional: paints and paintbrushes, scraps of paper, glue

1. **Simply use the masking tape** to affix a mixture of loo roll tubes and cut open kitchen roll tubes directly along the chosen wall at heights that your children can reach.

2. **Place a little bowl** or egg carton at the bottom of the run to catch your stone or marble in.

3. **Sometimes we tape our rolls to a big piece of cardboard** instead of the wall. This way, it can be propped up for play but then slid behind the sofa for another day.

FAMILY FAVOURITES

Making personalized versions of your favourite puzzles and games is an easy and creative outlet and often more fun can be had with a customized game than with a standard store-bought version. This way, you can tailor each puzzle or activity to suit your family and add personal touches that bring joy and build memories.

Packet puzzles

This craft project combines my love for making things out of scraps and Lily's love of puzzles. Of course, puzzles are a great way to keep occupied indoors, all together, or even solo. By using empty packets, you can put a lots of empties to use while making a variety of different puzzles to entertain you and your little ones.

What you will need
- 2 identical empty packets with a pattern
- Scissors

1. **Cut the sides of the packets** you are using away from the rest of the box. One of the packet sides becomes your guide so set this aside.

2. **Cut the other packet side into pieces.** To complete the puzzle, place the pieces on top of your guide.

3. **The older your child** (or your adult – I cut up a beer box into tiny pieces for Stu) the more pieces you can cut! I started with six large pieces, when Lily was just two. As she improved, I cut these pieces in half and then in half again.

Sports roulette

One weekend, Stuart and I decided to throw a sports day in the living room. We gathered all the sporting equipment we had, and set out spaces to play and to teach Lily the basics of various games. In a marriage of my creativity and Stuart's sportiness, we put together a roulette board featuring various aerobic activities in order for our whole family to do circuits. Even now, this is still a favourite activity, played in the living room, usually with a great playlist on in the background to keep rhythm.

What you will need
- Marker pen
- Large cardboard sheet (the bigger the better, to add to the drama and fun of the spinning game)
- Kitchen roll tube or empty bottle

1. **Using the marker pen,** draw a large asterisk shape on your cardboard sheet to split out sections.

2. **Fill the sections** with your chosen actions. Some ideas we use include: boxing, star jumps, jumping jacks, burpees, lunges, hop on left leg, hop on right leg, skip around the room.

3. **Decide on a number of repetitions** for each of these activities – you might prefer to have a different number for adults and children or just choose a different number each round, as we do.

4. **Use an empty kitchen roll tube** or bottle as your spinner. The bottle is the preferred option in our house but, of course, this depends on the ages of your young ones and the surface you're playing on. Spin your spinner, watch it land on an action and move!

5. **As mentioned, we put music on** in the background and have great fun moving to the beat. You could include breathing exercises or yoga positions as actions for something slow and calming, too.

Make your own memory game

This is another homemade version of a game that is adored by Lily and was inspired by her favourite things. There is something about these custom-made, just-for-you versions that is so pleasing and special. You can make this alone for your child or together with them. A personalized memory game is also a lovely present for your child to make and gift to a friend. In the same way as standard memory games, the idea is to match up the squares by turning over two at a time, replacing them face down if the images do not match, and then playing on, while trying to keep in mind where the corresponding pairs are. I also love the fact that you can keep adding to your game, with more hand-drawn pairs over time. It's an ever-growing game for ever-growing little ones.

What you will need:
- Cardboard sheet
- Colouring pencils or crayons
- Scissors (or craft knife)
- Optional: ruler

1. **Cut the sheet of cardboard** into similar sized squares.

2. **For Lily's favourites version,** I requested a little list of some of her favourite things. Sketch out pairs of the items on your cut up squares. Your little one can colour them in if they like.

3. **Turn them upside down,** mix them around and play.

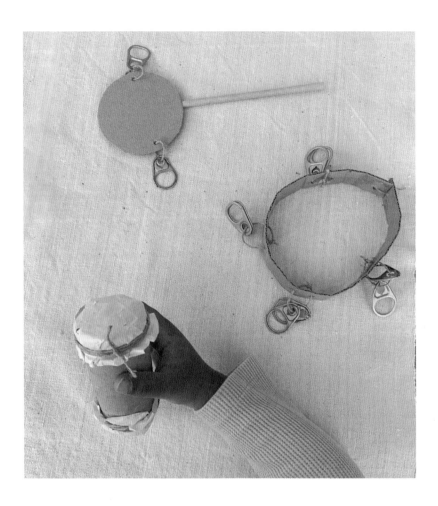

MAKE YOUR OWN MUSICAL INSTRUMENTS

We love family dance sessions in our house. In fact, it is a rare weekend that passes by without one. While you don't need anything for a family dance session save each other and a great playlist, some little percussion instruments are fun to make and fun to play with.

Maracas

For independent little crafters, this one can largely be made by them on their own.

What you will need:
- Scrap paper (or baking paper, scrap fabric)
- Loo roll or kitchen roll tubes
- Small handful of rice (or pasta, dried beans)
- Scissors
- Tape or twine

1. **Prepare by cutting out two circles** from your scrap paper or fabric. The circles need to be larger than the circumference of your loo roll tube.

2. **Next, your child can decorate** their tube, if they'd like. Once decorated, have them tape, or tie tightly with twine, one of the cut circles to one of the tube ends.

3. **Fill the tube with rice** through the open end.

4. **Lastly, secure the other circle** to the other end of your tube with tape or tie with twine to seal the rice inside. Shake away!

MAGAZINE OR OLD NEWSPAPER 'I SPY'

For those of you like me, with stacks of magazines you can't bring
yourself to pass on or coffee table books you've yet to read cover to
cover, this game is a way to make use of them. A twist on the classic
'I Spy', this game is best enjoyed on the sofa, with your little one
tucked in one arm, a beverage in the other and your magazine or
book on your lap. Simply take turns in playing 'I spy' for sights
among the pages. If your children are still a bit young for 'I spy', then
swap the alphabet for colours, people or animals – things that they
can easily identify until they're at the stage of using letters. For
numbers practice, we also play 'I spy three yellow things' and so on.
The beauty of this game is that through studying the pages of a book
or magazine, your children may catch sight of things they wouldn't
usually see: different foods in recipe books, different landscapes in
travel magazines and more of the world that's out there.

SCAVENGER HUNT

This is a simple but effective idea to send little ones off hunting safely
indoors while you oversee, perhaps with your feet up, nearby. Draw a
quick sketch of items around the room for your children to find. My
suggestion would be easily portable, non-fragile items, so that they
can bring them to you and you can tick them off. Don't worry about
your sketching skills – it's funny to draw something that they just
cannot decipher and see what ends up being brought back! If you
have a little one of reading age, this could also be a great way to
encourage some reading with labels in addition to, or instead of,
the drawings.

Tambourine

If your little one enjoys threading activities, this is a great one for them. It's another slow craft that you can revisit time and again, too. Most likely (unless you've been collecting), you won't have an abundance of ring pulls squirreled away from tins or cans and stashed somewhere. So, you can add as you go, building on your tambourine as you come across more ring pulls.

What you will need
- Cardboard sheet
- Ring pulls from canned drinks or tin cans (we used 12 for the last tambourine we made)
- Twine or string
- Scissors
- Optional: a glass, a pencil, holepunch

1. **Begin by cutting a wide strip** of cardboard from the sheet. Roll the strip into a circle shape. I wrap mine around a glass to achieve this and then open it back out to the size I want. Then pierce a hole at each end of the strip.

2. **Poke or pierce pairs of holes** at intervals around the strip. You want two holes next to each other, but not so close that they amalgamate into one hole. I remember once piercing a hole with the point of my scissors and then forcing the end of a paintbrush through as I didn't have a holepunch, so use whatever you have at home.

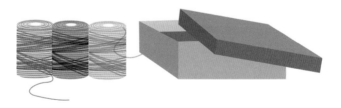

3. **Cut some short lengths of twine** – as many lengths as you have pairs of holes.

4. **Thread a length of twine** through two ring pulls. Very young ones may be able to do this as the holes are quite large, but be sure to check beforehand for any sharp metal edges.

5. **Next, thread each end of the length of twine** through each hole of the pair (or again have your helper thread). Pull the twine through and tie on the inside of the strip. Then tie together the two ends of the strip to secure the tambourine together.

6. **Trim any overhangs** and give this a little jangle (for a sound check!).

7. **Repeat this process** until you run out of ring pulls or holes. You can always add more later on.

Rattle drum

If you'd like to make an instrument but can only locate two ring pulls then this craft is for you! The real fun of this instrument is in how it is played. It's a simple craft that children can really make their own through decorating and then use in such a playful way. They have to place the stick handle in the palm of one hand, pressing their other hand on top and rubbing their hands back and forth.

What you will need:
- Small scrap of cardboard
- 2 x ring pulls
- Straw or stick for handle (a spare chopstick from a takeaway meal also works well)
- String or twine
- Tape

1. **Cut a circle** from the cardboard scrap. I use a roll of tape as a guide for this and cut around it.

2. **Pierce two holes** at opposite edges of the circle (if you were looking at a compass, you would be piercing the west and east positions). This can now be decorated by your child as they wish.

3. **Once decorated,** cut two lengths of twine. Thread one length through each ring pull. As with the tambourine, threading in this way is a great starting point for young ones as the holes are so big. Do be sure to check beforehand for any sharp metal edges.

4. **Attach each ring pull** to a hole in the cardboard circle by threading the twine through the holes and tying them in a knot. Don't make the loops too long or too short even – the distance between the ring pull and the cardboard circle should be about the size of the ring pull itself.

5. **Take whatever you are using** as a handle – a chopstick, a stick, a straw – and tape this to one side of your circle. Twist the handle to make the ring pulls move back and forth, hitting the cardboard and make some music!

CELEBRATIONS AND DECORATIONS

This section is dedicated to all things celebration, with some wonderful crafts to get stuck into in the run up to special days and holidays, or just to bring a bit of sparkle to your space.

'Thank you' cards

I often turn my girls' artwork into cards for family and friends. I'll cut out or around their drawings and paintings and stick them onto folded paper cards, keeping them in a cupboard for special occasions. Cutting shapes or letters from their colourful abstracts makes for wonderful, homemade stationery! Intentionally setting out to make cards together is a special way to spend time, too. I remember Lily and I making a set of thank you cards for all the people that came and went from our house one day. We left a card taped to the letterbox for the postman, and another taped to the recycling for the bin men, and then waited and watched from the window as they collected our little handmade surprises. Cut postcards or fold cards for your child to decorate as they wish. They can be for a particular occasion but also kept to give at a later date. It's a good opportunity to talk about special days, showing love and giving thanks. This is also a great creation to add pressed flowers to (see page 198).

Flower vase

I first saw this being made by an illustrator I follow online. I loved it and bookmarked it to try with the girls. As I write this book, I think about the fact that my ideas will (I hope) be bookmarked, too. It makes me so happy to imagine! It's incredible that through writing and posting, or even just sending pictures of our kids enjoying a particular craft to friends, we are able to share and inspire other families with creations that we have enjoyed.

What you will need:
- 2 cardboard sheets
- Flowers with thin stems (daisies from the garden or sprigs of herbs)
- Scissors
- Glue
- Optional: colouring pencils, paint

1. **Take one cardboard sheet,** which will be used for details, and cut out a vase shape. I cut freehand as I like the freedom of creating this way, but you may prefer to draw an outline and cut around it. This can be decorated however you choose.

2. **Stick the vase shape** to your second cardboard sheet.

3. **Using your vase as a guide,** poke holes in the second sheet in various places.

4. **If necessary, trim the stems of your flowers,** before poking them through the holes in your cardboard, which completes the craft. Lily really enjoyed doing this bit.

Post box

As ever, with children, the simplest things often bring the most delight and this craft truly demonstrates that, given that it takes no time at all to make and is created from only one item. I first made it for Willow, when she was around ten months old. Like many little ones of that age I'm sure, she was a huge fan of posting things and still is. This can also add something special to celebrations – bringing it out for birthdays makes for more magic than simply retrieving letters from the door mat or box in the hall. It doesn't have to be just birthdays either, but can be used before other celebration days, too. Creating the post box is quite simply making two holes in a box. You may want to turn your box inside out, if it has a design on it and you'd prefer a blank canvas to decorate. For my super quick way of doing this, see page 15 in the Creative Notes section of the book.

What you will need:
- Cardboard box
- Scissors (or craft knife)
- Tape

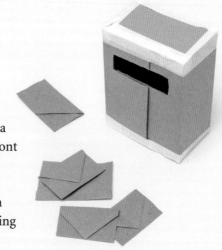

1. **Using scissors** or a craft knife, cut a letter-shaped window out of the front of your box, near the top.

2. **On the back side of the box,** cut a cat flap shaped opening for retrieving the posted letters and cards.

3. **Decorate the box** as you wish.

Birthday bunting

My wonderful online community with whom I am forever sharing little thoughts, crafts and ideas will know of our birthday traditions for the children and my love of the children's special days. As I've written before, it's not that we do anything huge, we just have some lovely traditions that bring me joy. One of these is birthday bunting. And, although we use it every birthday, its simplicity means it can be thrown together at a moment's notice, in readiness for any and all last-minute occasions.

What you will need:
- 2 cardboard sheets
- Twine or string
- Scissors
- Tape
- Things to decorate (colouring pencils, paints, petals or scrap paper pieces, glue)

1. **Cut out triangles for flags** or letters to spell out names or messages, or any shape you like, from your cardboard.

2. **Decorate these as you wish.** We are big fans of painting here, especially when using letters.

3. **Make loops out of little lengths of twine** and tape them to the back of each flag or letter. Thread these onto a longer length of twine. The little lengths can be re-used again and again for bunting, and the threading is a great skill for children to practise. Alternatively, affix the flags or letters directly onto the twine using tape.

THE GROWN-UP'S ROOM

We have co-slept with the girls on and off since they were born. We did settle them into their own bed and cot at one stage, but then we moved to France and so back to our bed they returned, to ease the adjustment of such a huge change. As such, it very much feels that our room has become an extension of theirs. Even now, when they do mostly sleep in their own room, they burst into ours first thing in the morning. If any of us are having days where we feel under the weather, it's our room that we cosy up in. So, it is here in this special space that we have come up with the games and crafts that follow.

PLAYING PARENTS

While they don't always do as I ask, say or suggest, my children very often do as I do. Perhaps this is also the case for you? I have seen much of my own behaviour mirrored in Lily and even Willow, although she's at a younger age. So, in the following pages you'll find a series of crafts and plays inspired by the 'mini me' in our life taking inspiration from us.

Make-up kit

This was a novel creation for both Lily and me. I'm not much of a make-up wearer these days and so had to dig deep in my memory for reference. For Lily, the absence of this in her mother's life meant she'd somewhat missed out on that glorious scene of little girls or little boys discovering their parent's make-up bag for the first time. While I am no whizz at make-up application, creating a cardboard kit, I can do. So, here's the starting point, which you can add to with replicas of your own must-haves.

What you will need:
- Cardboard sheet
- 2 x loo rolls tubes
- Twine or string
- Kitchen foil
- Scissors (and craft knife, if you have one)
- Tape (and glue, if you have some)

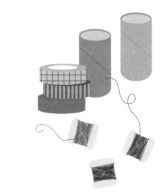

FOR THE COMPACT POWDER AND MIRROR (A)

1. **Cut two circles** of the same size from the sheet of cardboard. Place one on top of the other and cut a straight slither off both to give a flat edge for them to meet.

2. **Secure with tape** on one side – the circles should open and close.

3. **Open the circles** and glue a smaller circle of cardboard onto one side (for the powder) and a smaller circle of kitchen foil on the other side (for the mirror).

FOR THE EYESHADOW SET (B)

1. **Cut two rectangles of the same size** from the cardboard sheet. Using a craft knife or the blade of your scissors, carve out a slim rectangle near to the edge on one of the longer sides of one rectangle.

2. **Glue or tape the rectangle** with the cut-out on top of your intact rectangle. This little cut-out shape is for your eyeshadow brush to sit snugly inside.

3. **Next, cut out some smaller rectangles** or squares for eyeshadow colours (perhaps consult at this point with your assistant as to their preference). Glue these down onto the rectangle.

4. **Take a length of twine or string** and wrap around your forefinger, middle finger and ring finger three times. Pull it off your hand and tie or tape it together at one end.

5. **Cut across the loop of twine** at the other end to create the strands of an eyeshadow brush.

6. **Finally, cut a square of cardboard,** a little shorter than your twine brush. Place the twine on top, with some strands hanging over the edge, and roll the cardboard around it as if rolling up a pancake. Tape this into place. Your eyeshadow set is complete.

FOR THE BLUSH BRUSH (C)

1. **The blush brush is created** in the same way as the eyeshadow brush, just on a slightly larger scale. Cut a vertical slit through the loo roll tube.

2. **Wrap the length of twine or string** around your forefinger, middle finger and ring finger. Do this multiple times to create a nice, thick

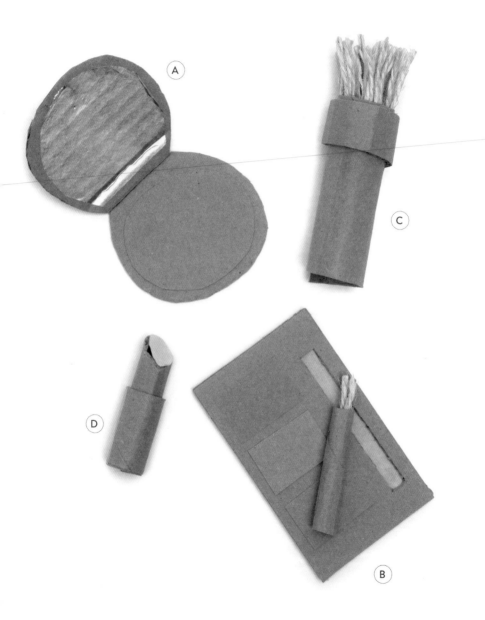

brush. I think I may have wrapped mine around my fingers about fifteen or so times!

3. **Carefully slide it off your hand** and tie or tape the loop together, very close to one end. Cut across the loop on the other end and you've made your brush head.

4. **Place this inside the cut-open loo roll tube** and tape to secure. Then, roll the tube as tightly as possible, like rolling a pancake, and tape again. For a little detail, cut another strip of cardboard and tape it across the edge where the brush and loo roll meet.

FOR THE LIPSTICK (D)

1. **To create a lipstick** that can be extended or shortened, first cut a small rectangle of cardboard. Roll this into a tube shape and tape in place.

2. **Using a craft knife or scissors,** carefully cut off the top of the roll at a diagonal angle – this gives you the lovely 'brand new' diamond shape of a lipstick. Later, this can be painted, or coloured in, in the shade of your little one's choosing. Or you could cover with a circle of tape, as we did.

3. **Cut a third off the remaining loo roll tube horizontally.** Cut the larger segment open vertically. Place your lipstick inside this, towards one end (it is just a holder). Roll the open loo roll tube back around this and tape. Don't tape it too tightly – leaving it a little loose allows you to push and pull the lipstick up and down.

4. **Lastly, take another square of cardboard** (or the remainder of your loo roll tube), and again wrap the almost complete lipstick inside this, taping it to secure.

PARENTS FANCY DRESS

I have more photos than I can count of Willow
sporting one of her dad's many hats and an oversized
sunhat of mine. At around the age of fourteen
months, she began to really express an interest and
ability in putting herself into clothes – pulling on
socks, putting on hats and sliding her legs into her
big sister's trousers. Alongside her, Lily would do the
same. Being taller, she was able to reach into our
wardrobe or open our drawers and not just access
the accessories left strewn around like Willow would,
but find t-shirts and cardigans, which she would pull
on and parade around the room in. This was never
an activity we would plan and was very much led by
the children. For a lot of fun, laughs and photo
opportunities, dressing or letting your children dress
themselves in some pieces from your wardrobe is a
great way to play.

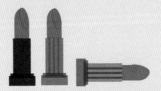

OLD BOX, NEW TRICKS

Glass jars and cardboard boxes are my two favourite things to re-use. From storage to craft items, I continue to find new ways to use them over and over. The two ideas in this section perfectly demonstrate the versatility of a humble shoebox.

Shoebox jewellery box

Transform an old shoebox into a keep safe for your little one's jewels. They can decorate it however they wish and fill it with their chosen accessories and trinkets.

What you will need:
- Shoebox
- Optional: cardboard sheet, tape or glue, scissors

1. **Add sections to the shoe box** by cutting strips from a cardboard sheet and gluing or taping them inside to provide compartments for rings, bracelets, necklaces and other treasures.

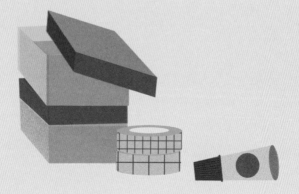

Shoebox time capsule

Creating a time capsule is one of my favourite things to do. I have countless photographs of my children on my phone, which don't get printed anywhere near enough, and mostly resurface yearly as a reminder of what I was doing 'on this day'. A time capsule is a different way to capture memories and one I began doing by chance. It was another early morning and I'd written a to-do list the night before, which I'd left on my bedside table. Lily bounded into our room before sunrise, scrambling across our bed, eagle eyed at the pen and paper in view. She started to doodle over my to-do list, before pausing and asking me to draw her a tiger – at the time, tigers were her absolute favourite. Having drawn my best 'Tiger who came to tea', I was then instructed to draw 'Daddy', 'wellies' and 'biscuits' – yet more of her favourite things. We labelled it 'Lily's favourites', dated it, then promptly forgot about it. It spent the weeks that followed as a coaster for my coffee. A few weeks later, when cleaning my room, I looked at it again properly. She had new favourite animals now, had discovered cake and was in summer shoes. I made a mental note that I'd ask her to tell me her favourites soon to note and date them. I put that note, and then the others that followed, in a shoebox in my wardrobe. Not all of the notes have favourites, sometimes they have a note about what she enjoyed for lunch, sometimes they have what she enjoyed doing at nursery. But all of them are dated, as a little reminder and capture of her at that moment in time.

What you will need:
- Shoebox
- Scraps of paper
- Pen or pencil

1. **You can decorate your shoebox** with your little ones to personalize each one. Add any mementoes, scribblings and drawings to the box as you go. Remember to date each entry as you go.

Loo roll jewellery

This craft was conjured up as a swift diversion of Lily's attention from my rings and necklaces, by creating some of her own. Her favourite items were the rings – maybe influenced by me because I wear so many. You can make lots of jewellery for your children to choose their own favourite, while filling their shoebox jewellery box (see page 86).

What you will need:
- Loo roll tubes
- Scissors
- Tape or glue
- Optional: cardboard sheet, twine

FOR THE RINGS

1. **Cut a loo roll tube open vertically,** before rolling it back again into a tighter tube, just wide enough for small fingers.

2. **Tape or glue** into place.

3. **Cut this newly created thinner tube** into horizontal segments to make a little collection of rings.

4. **You could also cut out** gemstone shapes from cardboard, decorate and glue these in place as a sparkly detail.

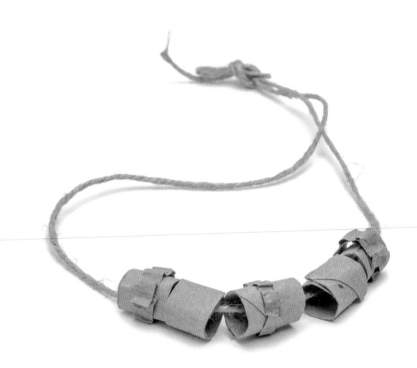

FOR THE NECKLACE

1. **To make a necklace,** first create beads from loo roll tubes: cut a tube open vertically, then roll it back in tighter to make a smaller, thinner tube and tape or glue in place.

2. **Cut this thinner tube** into horizontal segments to create beads. Now is a good time for your children to decorate them as they wish. They can also decorate some cut-out cardboard details if they'd like.

3. **Next, cut a length of twine** to fit your child's neck and thread the beads onto this. They may like to do the threading as the loops are so large – it makes good practice for dexterous little fingers.

4. **If you have cardboard details to add,** then tape them into place on the twine now, too.

FOR THE CUFFS AND BANGLES

1. **Cut open some loo roll tubes vertically**
   – this allows for them to simply slide over
   your little one's wrists.

2. **To create two cuffs,** cut one of the open
   tubes in half horizontally. You will have a
   nice big surface area here for your child
   to decorate as they wish.

3. **For bangles,** cut your open tube into
   thinner horizontal strips.

LEARN TO SEW

For Lily's third birthday, I found her a little pack of children's needles so that I could start teaching her to sew. The children's clothes are so often getting caught on branches and frayed or ripped at the knees and when I reassure Lily that we will mend them, she'll often ask me how. If your little one is interested in threading or mending, this makes for a good introduction. Take a sheet of cardboard and poke holes through. I do identical rows of holes and columns. The size of the holes you need will depend on the age of your young one, and also the thickness of your twine or string. Essentially, the younger the child, the bigger the hole. For thick holes use a pencil to poke through your holes. Then tie a length of thread, twine or string at the end of a cocktail stick and very tightly knot, and you're ready to sew.

Laptop

A cardboard laptop is a craft well worth creating. If it's used anywhere near as much as it is in our house, it'll be pulled out time and time again for months and months to come. It will also very likely have keys picked off and require countless repairs, too. But rather their cardboard laptop than your actual one! It's been so sweet to watch Lily mimic working alongside her dad and me, and sweeter still to see her joined by a Willow-sized colleague!

What you will need:
- 2 cardboard sheets (we used a cardboard envelope from a delivery of books)
- Scrap cardboard (for keys)
- A pen or pencil
- Scissors
- Tape
- Glue

1. **Tape the cardboard sheets** together along one edge, so as to create a book. Turn your book on its side.

2. **Cut seventy-eight keys** (or however many on your laptop – this was the number on mine) and add the characters to each with a pen or pencil.

3. **Older children may be able to do this themselves** by copying but you can help young ones, and they can assist by gluing each key in place, either by copying or following prompts from you.

4. **Remember to also cut out a cardboard rectangle** and glue this down for a trackpad in the centre towards the bottom edge.

Camera

Another 'grown up' item that is really popular in my house is the homemade camera. The first time I ever made one for Lily I really went to town on it. Crafting from loo roll tubes and cardboard, I spent an evening constructing it to include working buttons, removable lens caps and covers, rotating lens, rotating aperture dial, on and off switch, viewfinder and detachable neck strap! It was so very intricate and creating it brought me such contentment and satisfaction. The idea was that she could mirror me using my SLR camera, which she was fascinated with. Months later, while house hunting in France, we spent a week at a wonderful B&B. One night, a family of five came to stay, with children of similar ages to Lily and Willow. It had been such a long time that the girls had been away from other young children and they were delighted to make friends. One morning, I gave all five children a cardboard *atelier* (workshop). The boys of the family were allowed to choose what they wanted to craft and, having seen some photos of our creations, they chose cameras. They each crafted their own camera using recycled bits we'd kindly been given by the owner of the B&B. In the absence of loo roll tubes, they used packing paper and bottle caps and constructed their own equally magnificent cameras. They left on their travels, cameras around their necks, so, so happy. My girls were equally happy, but I think that was mostly for having met them. It was a glorious reminder of how children can find magic in the simplest of things.

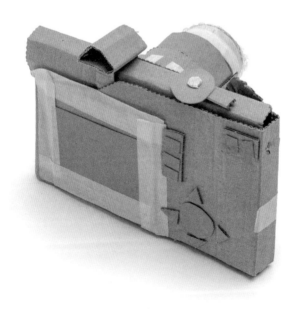

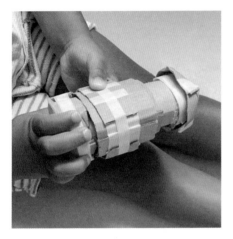
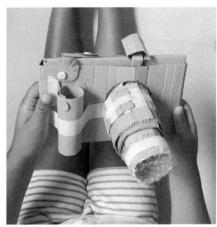
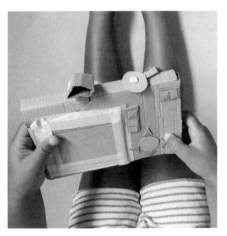
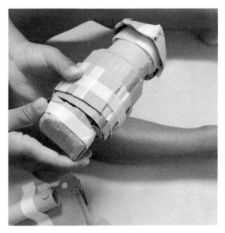

What you will need:
- Cardboard sheet or small cardboard box
- Bottle caps, loo rolls or lids (for the large lens)
- Bottle caps or scrap cardboard (for the aperture dial)
- Twine, ribbon or string (for the neck strap)
- Scissors
- Tape or glue

1. **Begin by preparing the base** for your camera by either cutting a rectangle from a cardboard sheet or using a rectangular shaped box.

2. **Affix a large lens** to your camera. You can do this simply by sticking down a circle of cardboard or by using a loo roll tube. For our camera, we cut a circle out of our camera base using our loo roll as a guide and then placed the loo roll into the hole. Tape another strip of cardboard loosely around the loo roll lens to give an element that can be turned.

3. **Continue to add more details.** For an aperture dial add a cirle of cardboard and a split pin. You can also add a viewfinder, by cutting a square out of your camera to see through.

4. **Remember to add** buttons and a display screen on the photographer's side, using whatever scraps you have.

5. **You can also add a length of string** so it can be worn around your photographer's neck! This is a particularly favoured detail in our house.

TRAVEL BAGS

I remember fondly the countless times I've watched Lily manoeuvre a cabin-sized suitcase that is twice the size of her, unzipping it and throwing in her essentials for an imaginary holiday. Nowadays, I watch a fifteen-month-old Willow circling the room with a large wicker bag of mine on her arm. One super long strap trails behind her and she stops intermittently to pack the bag with stray objects she finds on the floor. The dog bowl goes in, a toy, a fork – such busyness and concentration in the name of packing. Little ones love to pack, so here are two crafts for them to make a bag or case of their very own. What you need and how you'll craft differs slightly depending on whether you'd like to make a suitcase or briefcase.

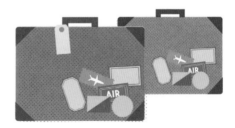

TRAVELLING STICKERS

There's something so nostalgic for me about a vintage suitcase covered with travelling stickers. They make me think of adventure, road trips and the great unknown. I spent a lot of time as a child wanting my own suitcase like that – my family and I travelled a lot but I never managed to gather an impressive collection. What I should have done, of course, was make my own! Prepare this by cutting out shapes from either cardboard or scrap paper. Cardboard works better for littler ones, as it is sturdier and more durable for them to hold and decorate. This is also a good opportunity to teach shapes to those keen to learn. Next, it's over to your little designer to draw and colour their own stickers. They could use photos from your trips as inspiration to create a sticker of somewhere they've already been to or a travel magazine for a sticker of a place they'd like to visit. Or better still, their imagination. These look great stuck down as decoration for your suitcase. This is such a nice craft to come back to in quiet moments or after you've been on a trip.

Briefcase

For both the briefcase and suitcase (see page 102), I turn the cereal boxes that I'm using inside out, so that the plain inside becomes the briefcase's outside and can be easily decorated by the children. The outside packaging then becomes the bag's lining. You can begin in this way too, or embrace or decorate on top of the outside packaging. I describe how I turn my box inside out on page 15 of the Creative Notes section.

What you will need:
• Cereal box
• Cardboard sheet
• Twine, string, ribbon or an old shoelace
• Scissors
• Tape
• Optional: drinking glass

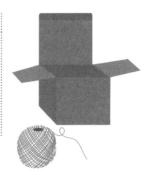

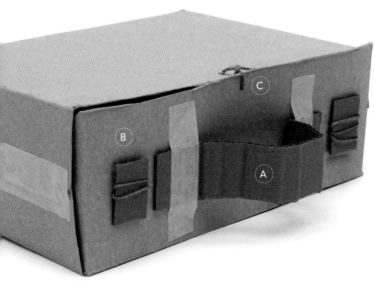

1. **Place the cereal box landscape** in front of you. If your cereal box is still open, tape the opening up to close it.

2. **Cut along one long edge** and two short edges of the top of your box with your craft knife or scissors. This will be the opening flap to the briefcase.

3. **Cut a length from the cardboard sheet** and wrap it around a drinking glass to curve it. Place this curved strip on top of the opening flap and tape each end in place. This creates your briefcase handle (A).

4. **You can also cut cardboard rectangles** for briefcase locks and stick these down on either side of your handle (B).

5. **Finally, poke a hole through the centre** of the briefcase top and the centre of the front face of the cereal box just below it.

6. **Cut a length of twine,** ribbon or an old shoelace and thread this through both holes. This allows you to tie and knot your briefcase to close it (C).

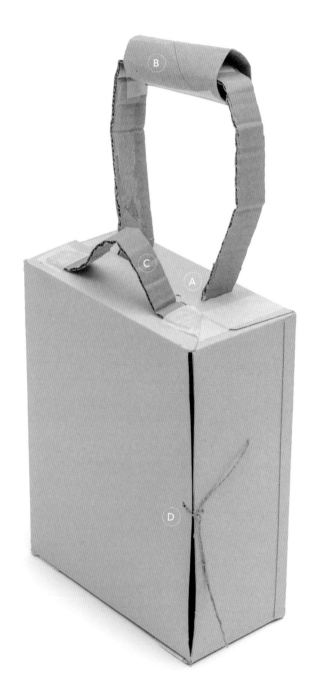

Suitcase

What you will need:
- Cereal box
- Cardboard sheet
- Loo roll
- Twine, string, ribbon or an old shoelace
- Scissors (and a craft knife, if you have one)
- Tape
- Optional: drinking glass

1. **Place the cereal box landscape** in front of you. Cut along the top front long edge with your craft knife or scissors, and then gently open up the sides of the box.

2. **The box will now open completely,** but you want to tape it together slightly to create the suitcase structure. Tape the smaller flaps of the box to the larger flaps (except for the opening you have cut) so that it takes shape as a box again.

3. **The side flaps of the front face opening** you have cut, can now slot into the taped together sides when the suitcase is closed.

4. **To create the suitcase arm,** cut two long strips from the cardboard sheet. Cut two horizontal slits in the left side of the cereal box suitcase (A) – the horizontal bit is important!

5. **These slits need to be wide enough** for your strips to slot into but not so wide that they can move too much when in place. The idea is that these can be adjusted up and down and stay in position, in the same way as with an actual suitcase.

6. **Slide the cardboard strips** into the horizontal slits. The flat sides of the strips facing each other. Tape them together at the top to create a little bridge.

7. **Cut open a loo roll tube vertically** and wrap this around the bridge to create an easy to grip handle (B). Tape into place.

8. **You can also add an additional fixed handle** by cutting a length of cardboard, wrapping it around a drinking glass to curve it and taping each end of this curved strip to the box below the suitcase arm (C).

9. **To finish, poke a hole through the centre** of the front and the centre of the side face of your suitcase. Cut a length of twine, ribbon or an old shoelace and thread it through. Use this to tie and knot your suitcase shut (D).

STORYTIME

I've always loved books. As a child, I was never without the
book I was reading – not only packing them in my book bag
for school, but also taking them on play dates and sleepovers,
and trips to the shops. I loved discovering new worlds through my books
and would become lost in them. Being such a love of mine, I was keen to
show my girls the wonder of books from a young age. But it was actually
through them that I discovered that books could offer even more than
the stories between their covers – and that even the simplest of board
books could be incorporated into play with the littlest of babies.

STORYBOOK HUNTING

When Lily was around two years old, she developed a fascination
with squirrels and getting her home from the park became quite
challenging due to her insistence on sitting and watching squirrels.
One day when we couldn't get out to the park to squirrel watch, I
decided we would go hunting through her storybooks instead. We
ended up happily squirrel hunting for ages. I gathered a huge
collection of her books and we flicked through all the pages,
spreading open and piling up the stories that had squirrel pictures in
and setting aside those that didn't. Lily would get so excited at finding
them – as would I! This is a go-to game for both girls as a change
from reading the same book cover to cover. I've always kept a basket
of books next to my bed for early mornings, so this is a game we
often play with them, picking a different subject to hunt each time.

Make your own storybook

What could be better for a storybook lover, than allowing them to create their own? This craft not only captures the brilliant minds of our children but is a wonderful way to develop language and stoke the fires of their imaginations. We mostly use scrap paper for this creation. It's very pleasing to see the backs of bills transformed into stories! Another thing: these books make a lovely addition to the shoebox time capsule featured on page 87.

What you will need:
- Scraps of A4 paper (or larger, cut down to size)
- Holepunch (or pencil to poke holes)
- Thread, twine or string for binding
- Pen or pencil

1. **Prepare the pages of the book** by folding A4 sheets of paper in half. Place these on top of each other – the more pages you use, the longer your storybook will be.

2. **Decide on your story** with your little one. This is my favourite part, seeing what they come with. You can write the story up for them and sketch some line drawing illustrations for them to colour in. Or perhaps they'll prefer to create the illustrations by themselves.

3. **Bind your book** by punching or poking holes at intervals through the spine. Thread short lengths of twine through two consecutive holes, knotting them in place.

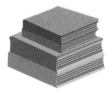

4. **Enjoy reading** this as a new bedtime story.

THE LITTLE ONE'S ROOM

Lily and Willow share a bedroom. Their walls are covered with crafts we have made together. In one corner sits a craft I've made for them, there's a small crate of books and a small crate of toys, and a huge old wardrobe filled with shelves and shelves of their clothes, which they mostly share too. Stepping into their room is like stepping into their world – special and magical and magnificently messy, all at once!

SMALL WORLD PLAY

Small world play is the creation of a miniature life scene through which our children can act, play, learn and explore. Small world play makes me think of Mary Norton's book *The Borrowers*. Little people having big adventures.

Doll's house

Our cardboard doll's house, like our cardboard oven (see page 46) is my replica of an heirloom one left behind in London. It sits in the girl's bedroom now, is so often played with and has needed very little in the way of repair over time. This is something I made for the girls, rather than with them, but would be a lovely craft to spend a series of days on with older ones. What I love the most about the doll's house is the endless possibility to craft. Cardboard window frames, scrap fabric curtains, hand-drawn views through windows and, of course, furniture. You can just keep adding and adding to this creation, and playing, too.

What you will need:
- Big cardboard box
- 3 large cardboard sheets
- Scissors (and craft knife if you have one)
- Tape
- Glue
- Optional: scrap paper, fabric, ruler

1. **Begin by creating 'the big door'** for your little ones to open and close their dolls house. Cut along the top, right-hand side and bottom edge of the front face of the box, leaving the left side attached so that door can open and close. If the front face of your box has flaps already, you can use these as double doors.

2. **Cut out windows** from the front face of the box. I use a ruler and a craft knife to cut squares for windows and once I've cut one, I use the discarded piece of cardboard as a stencil for the others to follow so that the windows are equal sizes.

3. **For the small door** (for the play people's entrance), use the same technique as for the big door – cut lines for the top, right-hand side and bottom of the door, folding back the left edge so that it open and closes.

4. **Now to create the floors.** Take a large cardboard sheet and cut it to a little longer than the width of the box. Fold the edges of this to fit the width and use tape to secure the folds to the insides of the box, creating the first floor. Take care to check that you've placed this in line with the windows by closing the big door and adjusting as necessary.

5. **Take a second large cardboard sheet** and cut this to a little longer than the height of the box. Fold the edges of this to fit the height. Before you tape in place, you need to cut a horizontal slit into the vertical cardboard sheet at the height of the first floor, so that the sheets slot together. This creates the division of rooms really simply.

6. **Tape as necessary to secure,** again taking into consideration the location of your little door – you don't want this opening straight into a wall!

7. **Using scrap cardboard from the trimmings,** or spare cardboard if you have some, you can now create steps. Zigzag fold a long strip of cardboard and fit to size between your floors. Make two of these if you'd like to create an attic floor.

8. **You can either tape this to the wall** of your house, or tape to a rectangle, folded in half, so that the stairs can be moved during play. Lastly, cut a square out of the horizontal first floor you've created, above your steps.

9. **Now to create the roof** and if you'd like, an attic floor. Take a third cardboard sheet and fold it in half. Sit this on top of your box, to give you an instant roof. Trim the sides to fit.

10. **Tape the roof in place.** If you only tape the back fold to the back of your doll's house box, you can lift open the front of the roof and use this space as an attic floor.

11. **Cut windows in the front face of the roof** and a square in the attic floor (the flat top of your box), so that your play people can move between floors. Your second set of stairs can be positioned here.

Puppet theatre

Turn a cereal or shoe box into a magnificent stage for puppets. Simple details, like curtains that open and shut and a stage backdrop, totally transform this craft into the perfect setting for a small-world play scene. I created an 'Under the Sea' themed puppet theatre at a time when Lily was fascinated by sea creatures. You can create whatever theme you like though – perhaps a secret garden, a circus or a living room.

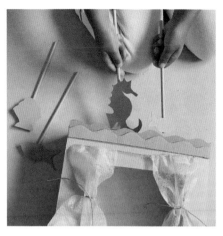
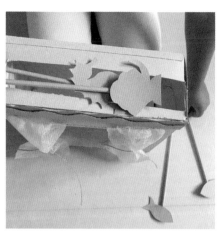

What you will need:
- Cereal box
- Scissors (and craft knife, if you have one)
- Scraps of fabric, cloth or paper
- String, twine or ribbon
- Tape
- Optional: scrap cardboard for details, glue

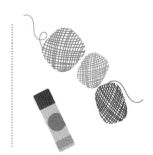

1. **Turn the cereal box landscape** and cut a large window out of the front face. Start this a quarter of the way from the top edge and cut down to the bottom, leaving approximately 5cm (2 inches) of cardboard either side. This creates your stage, with the space at the top allowing for your curtains.

2. **Cut a narrow window** in the top side of the box (A). This is the space from which you can poke your lollypop stick puppets through.

3. **Decorate the theatre if you wish** – don't forget to decorate the floor of your stage too.

4. **Now to add the details** that really transform the theatre. On the front face, pierce a hole in each side of the cardboard above the stage. Thread a piece of twine between the two holes, taping the ends of the twine on the inside (B).

5. **To create curtains,** cut a scrap of paper (or fabric – we used some lovely crepe paper that came in a parcel), the same width as your stage window but a little longer in length. Cut this in half to make two curtains (C).

6. **Roll the top of one curtain around the twine** and tape or glue it back onto itself, leaving enough of a gap for the curtains to move freely along the twine and to slide back and forth. Repeat with the second curtain.

7. **Cut two more lengths of twine** to tie the curtains around the middle when your show is in session.

Lollypop stick puppets

These puppets are a perfect companion to the previous project, the Puppet Theatre (see page 116). This is a lovely craft for you to start and your little one to finish, creating their own unique characters for their puppet theatre.

What you will need:
- Cardboard sheet
- Lollypop sticks (or straws or strips of cardboard)
- Scissors
- Tape

1. **Cut out silhouette shapes** of your choice from the cardboard sheet, as directed by your young theatre producer. We created sea creatures for our 'Under the Sea' theatre theme.

2. **Decorate the shapes** with facial features, clothes and colour.

3. **Tape the finished creatures** to the bottom of the lollypop sticks, strips or straws and get playing!

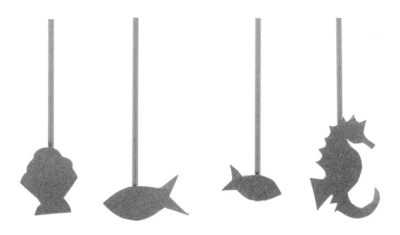

Loo roll finger puppets

Finger puppets are fantastic, theatre or no theatre. We use them in our house regularly for roleplay and exploring emotions with the girls.

What you will need:
- Loo roll tubes (or kitchen roll tubes)
- Scrap paper
- Scissors
- Tape
- Pencil
- Optional: glue

1. **Take a loo roll or kitchen roll tube** and cut into segments horizontally. I tend to cut the loo roll tubes in half and kitchen roll tubes into four.

2. **Cut each segment open vertically** and roll into a tighter tube to fit your fingers (or your children's fingers). Tape in place to secure.

3. **Draw a puppet character** on a piece of scrap paper – perhaps a family member or animals. The first time we did this we drew various circus animals, giving them all red top hats. We prefer to stick with just faces and necks, the necks being the same width as the puppet tube, but you can draw entire bodies if you prefer.

4. **Cut out your characters** from the paper and glue or tape onto the finger tubes.

MAGIC AND MAKE-BELIEVE

The benefits of imaginative play for our children are abundant. Play in this way gives our children a safe place to explore emotions, empathy, negotiation and real-life situations. Magic and make believe allows them to explore concepts outside of day to day life, too. It's incredible to hear and witness their creativity and the realms of their imaginations when playing with a little magic.

Castle

When Lily was just two years old, I stayed up late one evening to make her a castle. I constructed it in such a way that she would be able to take it apart and rebuild it herself. I made cardboard turret tops to fit over loo roll tower tubes, plaited drawbridge ropes from twine to be hung on top of columns made from taped cocktail sticks and hung fabric flags on top of masts also made from cocktail sticks. She loved it so much, putting it together a little differently each time and making up adventures for her play people. And I loved that it could be packed away into one box and brought out as if it were a new toy every time.

What you will need:
- Cardboard box
- 4 x loo roll tubes
- Scissors (and a craft knife, if you have one)
- Tape or glue
- Optional: egg cartons, cocktail or lollypop sticks, scrap paper or fabric

1. **To create the castle structure,** begin by taking the top off the box and setting the cardboard aside to use for details later on.

2. **Cut gaps out along the top edge** of the box to create battlements along the walls (A), which instantly begins the castle transformation.

3. **Tape or glue the loo roll tubes** to the four corners of your box to create towers. Should you wish to pack your castle away and play another day, cut a slit in the tube instead of gluing it on, so that you can slide the towers on and off the wall (B).

4. **Egg carton cups make great roofs for towers,** or you can cut battlement strips from your set-aside cardboard and wrap them around the tops of the towers. Tape them in place (loosely, if you want to slide them on and off).

5. **Cut windows out of the cardboard walls** using your scissors or a craft knife.

6. **Cut out a door.** You may wish to add a drawbridge from your scrap cardboard (C). Glue or tape lengths of twine between the drawbridge and castle door.

7. **You can add to the castle over time.** Zigzag folded steps within the castle, circular cut-out peep holes in the walls or a smaller box 'Castle Keep' placed inside. I often refer to the girl's picture books when crafting for inspiration and so that they make links between what they see and how they can play.

8. **To make a flag,** cut out a diamond from scrap paper or fabric and fold it in half to make a triangle. Open the diamond up again and glue a cocktail or lollypop stick along the folded line. Add more glue to one triangle and stick both triangles together. These can be poked into tower roofs or stuck alongside the drawbridge.

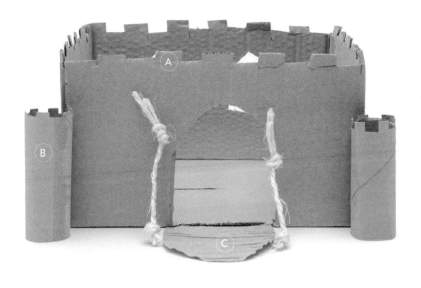

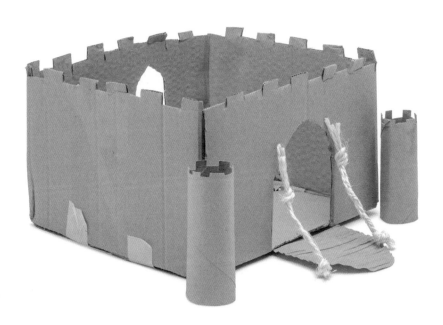

Fairy wings

The first time that I tried to make fairy wings for Lily will be etched forever into my memory. It was hilarious and totally epitomized her character at aged two: fun-loving and wonderfully cheeky. I couldn't get the armbands right on the first version of the wings. I had used strips of cardboard and wrapped them around her tiny shoulders using copious amounts of tape to affix them to the wings, but it didn't work at all. Lily kept 'flying away' mid adjustment and so the wings would fall off and I was left exasperatedly chasing after her with more tape and more cardboard. I have photos from that afternoon of Lily wearing the finished wings with a big wide smile and glittering eyes, full of joy. One morning, a few weeks later, Lily came to me and said 'Mum! I need my butterfly wings! I need to fly!' So, after a bit of hunting, I found the wings we had made, and as if by magic, also found an ingenious (and much simpler way) for the wings to be worn.

What you will need:
- Cardboard sheet
- Ribbon or twine
- Scissors
- Optional: pencil

1. **Fold the sheet of cardboard in half** and cut out half a silhouette of fairy wings.

2. **Open the cardboard up** and pierce a hole in the middle of each half, close to your fold line (A).

3. **You or your little one can decorate the wings** as you wish now.

4. **To wear, cut two lengths** of twine or ribbon. Fold the twine in half to create a loop and thread the two ends from the inside of the wings to the decorated side.

5. **Twirl and knot the ends together.** Your little one's arms will go through the loop on the other side and the twine can be adjusted so that the wings fit comfortably and securely!

Magic wands

This is another easy go-to for endless magical play. Both Lily and Willow love these wands, and we bring them out for all manner of occasions.

What you will need:
- Cardboard sheet
- Straw (or lollypop stick or kitchen roll tube)
- Scissors
- Tape
- Optional: foil or empty crisp packets

1. **Cut a star shape** from the cardboard sheet and allow your magician to decorate it, if they wish.

2. **Tape a straw** or stick to one side of the star to create your wand handle.

3. **If using a kitchen roll tube,** cut it open vertically, roll it in tighter and tape again to secure. Tape this to the back of the star.

4. **You could cut strips of foil** or cut up an empty crisp packet, if you have one, and tape these to the back of your star to add a little sparkle.

Superhero Costume

I love crafts like this as they really impress our kids. I think for this craft in particular, it's the combination of all the little features – a costume complete with facemask, belt, cape and cuffs – all to be customized exactly as they wish! As you complete each piece of the costume, your child can begin decorating it to make their unique Superhero costume.

What you will need:
- 2 x cardboard sheets
- 2 x loo roll tubes (don't worry if you only have one)
- Twine
- Bin bag or large scrap of paper (wrapping paper or easel paper work well)
- Twine
- Scissors
- Optional: scrap paper and glue

FOR THE FACEMASK (A)

1. **Cut out an eye-mask shape** from a cardboard sheet. Measure it against your little one's face before carefully piercing out eye holes with the scissors.

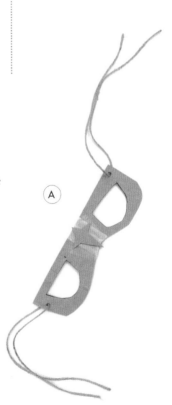

(A)

2. **Poke a hole through** each side of the mask.

3. **Feed a length of twine through each hole** and knot in place, so the mask can be tied at the back of their head.

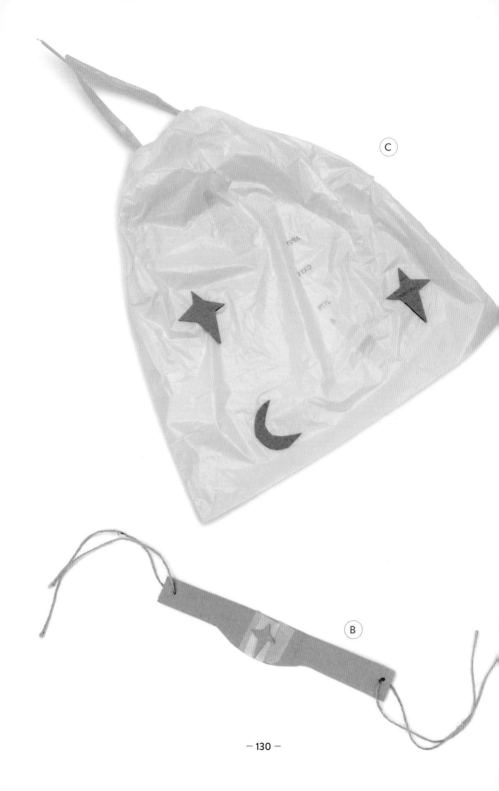

C

B

FOR THE BELT (B)

1. **Cut a long, thick rectangular strip** from the second cardboard sheet.

2. **Poke a hole through** at each end of the strip.

3. **Feed a length of twine** through each hole and knot in place, so the belt can be tied around your little one's waist.

FOR THE CAPE (C)

1. **My easiest go-to for a cape** is an unused bin bag with drawstrings, and when it's been worn out, it can be used as a bin bag as usual! Pull the drawstrings in tight, tying them in a large loop so they can be worn around the neck. Your little one can also decorate it with scraps of paper and glue.

2. **Alternatively, a large sheet of paper** (such as brown wrapping paper) can be used for a more delicate cape. Cut a semi-circle out at one end of the paper, leaving space to feed through a length of twine through two poked holes on each side of the semi-circle. This can then be worn around your little one's neck after their decoration.

FOR THE CUFFS (D)

1. **Cut the loo roll tubes open** vertically so that it can be worn around a wrist. If you only have one, cut it in half for smaller – but no less super – cuffs. Add cut out decorations as desired.

Prince and princess crowns

We love cardboard crowns in our house – they are just so versatile. They can be used as birthday crowns, prince and princess crowns at playdates and even crowns for our homemade crackers at Christmas. The best part about them: they take no time at all to put together. For king or queen crowns rather than prince or princess ones – you just need to give your crowns more height.

What you need:
- Cardboard sheet
- Scissors
- Twine (or string or ribbon)

1. **First, cut a rectangular strip** of cardboard of the approximate length of the circumference of your little one's head. It doesn't matter if it's a little short or a little long, as you secure the crown using twine and ribbon and therefore it can be adjusted.

2. **Cut zigzags on one edge** for the top of the crown.

3. **Poke a hole through** each end of the strip, thread a length of twine through each one and knot in place.

4. **Wrap the crown around** your child's head and tie the lengths of twine together.

5. **This can be decorated** by you or them for the occasion!

TAKING CARE OF BABY

Watching the girls play with their dolls or teddies is one of the cutest things. Of course, when playing this way, they're practising empathy and responsibility, skills to go out into the big wide world with, but what I love best, is their modelling of behaviour they've seen or been shown. It's this that I find so adorable.

Cradle

As shown throughout this book, and by our children too, a cardboard box can be many things. Add wheels and it becomes a car, add a blanket and it's a bed, and add a blanket, two loo roll tubes and two more strips of cardboard and it's a cradle that rocks!

What you will need:
- Cardboard box
- Cardboard sheet
- 2 x loo roll tubes
- Scissors
- Tape or glue
- Optional: another cardboard sheet

1. **Begin by taking the lid off** the box.

2. **From the cardboard sheet,** cut two vertical lengths. These will need to be about one and a half times the width of the box so that you will be able to create a curve. If you have any cardboard left over from the sheet, set it aside to use later on.

3. **Wrap the two strips** around the loo roll tube to curve them. These two arcs will be the feet that allow the cradle to rock back and forth.

4. **Turn the box upside down** and place the arcs across the width of the box (horizontally) at each end (A).

5. **Next, take the two loo roll tubes** and cut slits around the rim of the tube on both ends. Fold these slits backwards towards the loo roll to create a flat surface.

6. **Place each roll in between** an arc and the underside of the cardboard box and tape in place across the bent backwards slits (B).

7. **Also tape the ends of the arcs** to the sides of the box.

8. **Turning the box upright** and placing it on the floor you should now be able to rock your box cradle back and forth!

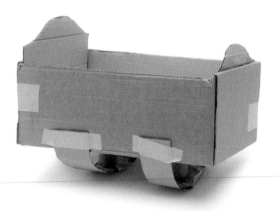

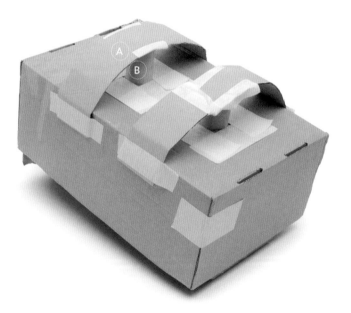

9. **Using the set-aside cardboard sheet,** or spare cardboard if you have some, cut out a headboard and footer for the cradle and glue to the inside of the box (C).

Baby doll or bear carrier

Both my girls love this replica of the baby carrier that they themselves were carried around in. I've made one for each of them and they look so cute, walking around with their bears strapped to their fronts, playing at being mum.

What you will need:
- Cardboard sheet
- Teddy bear or doll
- Scissors
- Ribbon (or twine or dressing-gown cord)
- Optional: holepunch

1. **Cut out a baby carrier shape** from a piece of cardboard. Adjust the size according to the dimensions of your doll/bear and the size of your little one.

2. **In order for it to be worn comfortably** again and again, use ribbon or twine to tie it. Pierce holes with your scissors on both sides of the carrier at the top and bottom.

3. **Thread the ribbon or twine through each hole** and tie in bows across your children's waist and shoulders. This can be adjusted to fit.

FEEDING BABY

There are so many glorious doll and baby accessories available for play right in your own home – just go on a little shopping spree through your own kitchen cupboards! Gather together feeding utensils, your child's old or current ones. Collecting them up could be done together, as a great way to talk about what baby might like to eat, how to protect babies' clothes and so on. Once you have everything, then you can get stuck into play. I love how children can get so lost in roleplay. Sometimes they'll need you to start them off with leading questions, but very often play is totally independent, leaving you to watch in wonder nearby.

DRESSING UP BEAR

Dig out some of your little one's baby clothes for them to use to dress up their favourite bear or doll. Lily loves hearing stories and looking at photos of herself as a baby in the same outfits.

ARTS AND CHARTS

These are some of my favourite crafts to teach time, days of the week and growth. There are some projects in here that have helped us with trickier times, such as periods when the girls were having difficulty sleeping. Many of these crafts have provided sustainable room décor, too!

Marking and measuring

A simple idea that I remember from my own childhood was having my height measured regularly and marked on the wall. I would stand with my back to the wall in the hallway of our house and one of my parents would make a mark in pencil on the wall above my head. They would add to the mark, either the date or my age in years and months. The memory is very hazy, but sweet enough for me to adopt this with my own children. I love the idea of doing this on the back of the children's bedroom door but understandably you may want to protect your walls. Instead, you can use a strip of paper-based or masking tape as a marker, which can be taken off and taken with you should you move home or they move rooms.

What you will need:
- Pencil
- Optional: paper-based tape or masking tape

1. **Have your little one stand** with their back to the wall and mark their height, either directly onto the wall or onto a piece of tape.

2. **Repeat when you remember** and enjoy commemorating and reminiscing over their constant growth in the years to come.

Superstar sticker chart

Soon after Willow was born, Lily, completely understandably, began having trouble going to sleep. Whereas before she would happily nod off alone after a story and cuddles, she now began to call out for us once we had left her room, tearful and asking that we stay with her. So, in order to give bedtime a positive association again, I made her a sticker chart, which we hung above her cot. Each morning we would give her a sticker and in turn, bedtime became relaxed again, with the promise and excitement of a sticker being added the next morning. A few months later we were travelling in France without Lily's sticker chart, so I made a sticker book instead and each day gave her a 'Superstar sticker'. She began to decide on the criteria for receiving a sticker, which ranged from 'being a brilliant girl' and 'being very kind' to 'just because'. I loved that it became a way for her to rightfully give herself praise!

What you will need:
- Cardboard sheet
- Colouring pencils, paint or scrap paper
- Stickers (or make your own from paper cut-outs and glue)
- Optional: tape and twine (to hang), ruler

1. **Take a large sheet of cardboard** and create a chart that suits your purpose. For my original sticker chart, I marked lines for the days of the week and added a border of stars. Think about how you'll use it with your child and design it and decorate it accordingly. Attach twine to be able to hang the chart if liked.

Days of the week chart

A quick and easy way to practise learning the days of the week with your children, this is also a cute creation that can be displayed on their bedroom wall. It can be incorporated into your morning routine by asking your little one what day of the week it is and referring to the chart.

What you will need:
- Cardboard sheet
- Clothes peg
- Colouring pencils or paint
- Optional: ruler or spine of a book, twine, tape

1. **Divide a sheet of cardboard** into seven sections using a pencil and ruler (or the spine of a hard book).

2. **Label each section** with the day of the week. Your little one might like to decorate the page with pencils or paint, colour code each day or, if they're older, draw pictures of the things that they do on certain days.

3. **Once your chart is decorated** – and dry, if you have painted – you can mark the day of the week with a clothes peg. I love that pegs can be used by children themselves, while they practise reciting the days of the week.

NIGHT AND DAY

The crafts in this section have been so helpful for our family for learning to tell the time, explaining the concept of day and night and improving the bedtime routine. Making them together provides a perfect opportunity to discuss all of this and more.

Night-time mobile

This is a gentle craft, that can also help with bedtime routines, if you're in need of that.

What you will need:
- Cardboard sheet
- Twine or string
- Coat hanger
- Scissors
- Optional: food packets and glue

1. **From the cardboard sheet,** cut out some shapes that represent night-time as decided by you and your child. For our mobile, we cut out various moon phases, as Lily was especially interested in the varying shapes of the moon at the time.

2. **Decorate all the shapes** as you wish.

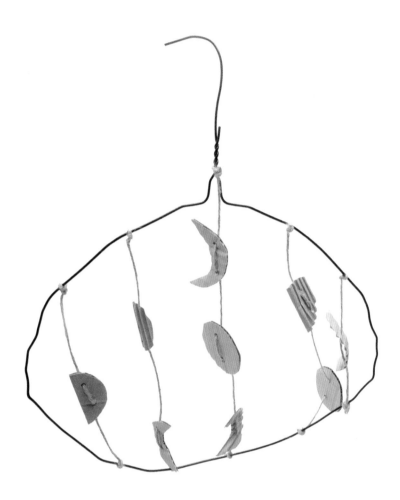

3. **Stretch the coat hanger** out to create a larger circle shape.

4. **Using scissors, poke a hole** at the top and bottom of each night-time shape and thread in sequence onto varying lengths of twine. You can decide how many strands of twine to use and how many shapes to add to each piece of twine.

5. **Tie the strands of twine** to the coat hanger and suspend from a hook or hang where suitable.

DIY clock

Making a clock with Lily was such a great tool to begin explaining the concept of time to her. Originally, instead of hours on the clock, I stuck cut-outs of food packets from different meals of the day to represent different times. I used a scrap of a baked beans packet for lunchtime, a scrap from a pot of yoghurt for snack time and a scrap from a pasta packet for dinnertime. I kept the night-time section blank when she ought to be sleeping. It worked really well and she quickly began to understand the phases of the day. For whatever age group, a homemade clock is a great resource, and can be customized with pictures, packets or paint – whichever they wish.

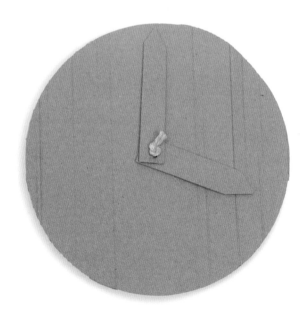

What you will need:
- Cardboard sheet
- Plate or bowl
- Scissors
- Split pin (or string or twine)

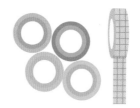

1. **Using a plate or bowl as a guide,** cut a circle shape out of the cardboard sheet.

2. **From the scraps of cardboard leftover,** cut out two arrows for the hands of the clock.

3. **Place the arrows in a clock position** on the circle of cardboard and pierce a hole with your scissors through the hands and clock face.

4. **Secure the hands to the clock face** with a split pin if you have one, so that you can spin the clock hands freely. (I have many split pins, although I can never find one when I need them!)

5. **Alternatively, feed a loop of string** through the holes and tie a knot in the front and back. Trim the lengths. You can now spin your clock hands in just the same way.

6. **Depending on the age of your child,** you can add pictures of food or numbers to the clock face to begin teaching them to tell the time.

THE BATHROOM

There's a beautiful quote on parenting that always comes back to me, which is 'when in doubt, add water and let them play'. The power of water to heal, restore and bring calm is not something to be overlooked. Water play is one of our go-to activities for those days when our girls are disgruntled, bored or restless, as much as it is for those sunshine-y, happy days. Within this chapter you'll find games for bath time, water-play time, and crafts for those times, too.

BATH-TIME BOATS

There are a number of ways to make boats that float for the bath. The following projects have either been discovered by chance following an overspill of breakfast plates into the sink, or hurriedly trialled to appease the girls' dissatisfaction at the obligation of bath time! There's also a classic in here that I just had to include.

Avocado boat

Happily, I discovered this after clearing up one of Lily's favourite meals to cook. (Side note – smashed avocado toast is a great dish for young children to make independently. If like us you enjoy yours with plenty of chilli, lemon and oil, this dish provides a great opportunity to be liberal and generous.) Anyhow, after haphazardly stacking the empty plates beside the sink, I was later given the idea for the avocado boat when half an avocado skin floated into my washing up bowl.

What you will need:
- Used avocado skin
- Spoon
- Scrap of paper
  or newspaper
- Cocktail stick
- Scrap of paper
- Glue

1. **To begin, take the used avocado** and gently scoop out any remaining flesh with a spoon. They can be quite tricky to get completely clean, so you may need to rinse in warm water and massage the inside of the skins. If you are not quite ready to use them, leave to soak in cold water and place in the fridge until you are.

2. **Once you are ready,** take a sheet of scrap paper and roll it up into a ball. Make as many of these as you have avocado skins.

3. **Next, make a flag.** Cut a diamond from a scrap of paper and fold it in half to make a triangle shape. Place the cocktail stick along the folded line.

4. **Apply glue to one side of the triangle** and fold over the other to glue together. Stick the flag into the ball of paper.

5. **Gently sit this in the avocado boat,** before placing it delicately in your bath of water.

Milk or juice box boat

If I had to pick, this boat would be my favourite. Not only did it have an entirely transformative effect on Lily, whose statement of 'I absolutely do not want a bath tonight' turned into 'Oh my word – this is so cool', but it is so simple you can go from juice box to sail boat in a matter of minutes.

What you will need:
- Juice or milk carton
- Lollypop sticks or takeaway chopsticks
- Scrap paper (tissue paper/ newspaper works well as very light)
- Scissors
- Glue
- Optional: colouring pencils or pens

1. **Rinse out a juice carton** or milk carton really well. I tend to fill halfway with warm soapy water, replace the lid, and shake vigorously (fun for kids to help with). This is an important step as unclean cartons make for unpleasant surprises and smells weeks later! Once your carton is clean, replace the lid.

2. **Pierce holes in the carton** with scissors. We made two holes for sails, but this of course depends on your little creator and the style of boat they envisage. Be careful not to make the holes too large. You want whatever you are using for the mast (lollypop sticks or chopsticks) to fit snugly inside the hole rather than 'bobbing' (pun intended) about.

3. **Add flags to the mast sticks.** Cut a triangle of tissue paper and stick onto lollypop sticks or chopsticks with glue. This is another opportunity for your little one to get stuck into design, by decorating the flag themselves.

4. **Slide the mast sticks** into the holes on the carton, ready to set sail.

Bottle cork boat

The bottle cork boat is a classic craft, which takes me back to my own childhood when I used to make these at school! There are lots of variations in method but this is the way we make them.

What you will need:
- 3 x corks per boat
- Twine, string or elastic bands
- Scrap of paper or fabric
- Cocktail stick
- Glue (superglue, if you are using material for the flag)

1. **Lay three corks together in a line.** If one of your corks is a champagne cork, and the others from wine bottles, then place this in the middle to ensure balance. If you have two champagne corks and one wine, place the wine cork in the middle.

2. **Secure the corks together across the middle,** using elastic bands or lengths of tightly tied twine.

3. **Take a piece of scrap paper** or fabric to prepare the flag. Cut a diamond from the paper or fabric and fold in half to make a triangle.

4. **Place a cocktail stick** along the folded line and glue the two halves of the triangle together.

5. **Finally, pierce the cocktail stick** through the middle cork in the boat. Now it's ready to set sail!

GIVE TOYS A BATH

Set up your little one with everything they need to give their toys a bath. Perhaps they will end up bathing with them or perhaps they can bath the toys alone in a small bowl. This is an effective way to encourage water play and practise bath time. I find the girls' concentrated little faces as they clean their treasured things so cute!

ICE, ICE BABY

We've found that simply adding ice is a great way to extend water play and add delight to a less than desired bath.

Frozen toys and frozen flowers

Freezing your little one's small toys to add to their warm bath can bring such joy. Our family all appreciate frozen flowers in our baths, so we do this, too. Lily helps fill up our ice-cube trays with wilting petals from a vase or flowers that we have foraged on walks. She is able to practise pouring from a jug, covering each petal with water and then leaves it in the freezer overnight, in anticipation of a fun-filled bath time the next day.

What you will need:
- Small toys, flowers buds or petals
- Kitchenware for freezing – (ice-cube trays, muffin trays, cake tins, sandwich boxes all work well).
- Water

1. **Add your child's favourite waterproof** toys, flower buds or petals to an ice-cube tray and cover in water.

2. **Pop into the freezer overnight** or first thing in the morning so that the ice cubes are ready for an evening bath and pop into the filled tub when ready to use.

Fruit and vegetable coloured cubes

Making coloured ice cubes is another effective idea for freezing games. There's not a lot of preparation involved with the frozen toys or flowers, but for little ones, making coloured cubes with fruit and vegetables is much like cooking. The end product brings wonderful pops of colour to your bath or water play. This is a great way to put to good use the dregs or sad-looking fruit or vegetables in your fridge. Please be sure to exercise caution when playing. While the cubes may be taste-safe, guidelines for children advise that young ones under four years old do not put ice cubes into their mouths. Similarly, for those with allergens or sensitive skin, I would avoid adding to a body bath, and instead add to a tub used simply for water play, with some spoons and towels nearby.

What you will need:
- Colourful fruits and vegetables (for pink, try strawberries or raspberries; for deep purple, use blueberries; for red, beetroot makes such a rich colour; for yellow, try saffron or turmeric; matcha or spinach work well for green; and tea is great for brown).
- Warm water
- Ice-cube tray
- Bowl, fork or potato masher

1. **Add a handful of your chosen fruit** or vegetable to a bowl and mash them using the back of a fork or a potato masher.

2. **Add drops of warm water,** a little at a time, to create a thick liquid. The thicker the liquid, the more intense the colour. If you're using powders or spices, I would add a spoon or two and add drops of warm water until you have a thick consistency.

3. **Fill your ice-cube trays** and freeze. These look so wonderful in water – I mix them up with some clear cubes, too.

HANDWASHING CLOTHES

Lily and I first adopted this slow pursuit one sizzling hot day. We needed something to cool us down but also needed more clothes to change into! It was a few days after extending a roadtrip through France, in search of a house, and we hadn't packed enough clothes. So, we bundled up some of our laundry and carried it up to the bathroom of the B&B we were staying in, the perk being that the weather was hot enough for the clothes to dry outside. For this, simply run a bath of warm water and add in your clothes. Make a game from this by getting your little one to either shout colours of the clothes or which family member each article belongs to before chucking it in. You or your child can pour in skin sensitive detergent before stirring all the clothes with a paddle. Rinse and wring out each item before hanging to dry. If you don't have a washing line, open a window, place a towel or blanket down and then place the clean clothes on top to dry.

SPLASH, PLAY (AND RE-USE)

A great many more of us are taking steps to avoid single-use plastics. While our family's efforts to do without these have improved significantly in recent years, there are still times that these items make their way into our home. To counteract this, I try to find ways to give them a little longer life and often end up using them for toys.

Shampoo bottle bowling

Save your shampoo bottles once they are finished to turn into bowling pins. Having ten pins to line up for ten-pin bowling is perfect but you can play this game with any number of pins. To add difficulty for older children, fill the bottles up with water to make them harder to knock over. We use a rolled-up piece of paper or sock as our bowling ball to ensure this is a break- and smash- free game, although you can use a small ball if you prefer.

What you will need:
- Scrap paper
- Red colouring pencil or paint
- Empty shampoo, conditioner or cosmetic bottles (not glass)
- Scissors
- Tape or glue
- Small ball (or rolled up sock or paper)

1. **Give your child a sheet of paper** to paint or colour with red pencil or paint.

2. **Once coloured,** cut the paper into long strips.

3. **Tape or glue two strips horizontally** around the top of each of your bottles to transform their appearance into bowling pins and bowl away!

FUN IN THE TUB

One of these games is not just reserved for bath time, instead it often fills up time on slow days with no plans. The other, my girls would play all night if they could. They play for so long that when they eventually clamber out of the bath, their fingers are shrivelled like prunes!

Tub of butter 'hook a duck'

This is a fun way to bring a bit of the circus to your bathroom and to use up leftover tubs from the kitchen.

What you will need:
- Scrap of cardboard
- Empty tub (butter and dairy tubs are our most used)
- Tiny toys that fit inside your tub (toy ducks are great – but anything can be used)
- Coat hanger
- Tape

1. **Cut out a strip of cardboard** a little larger than the length or diameter of your empty tub.

2. **Tape the cardboard strip into place** at each end of the tub to create a handle.

3. **Float the tub in your bath of water** and gently place your duck, toy or whatever you're using inside.

4. **Use the coat hanger as a hook** for the game. If it's a wire hanger, it can be bent into shape to make a more effective hook.

Yoghurt pot basketball hoop

This is a really fun game for your children's bath time, although most of the time it ends up with all of us soaked through!

What you will need:
- Large yoghurt pot
- Scissors
- Tape
- Small ball (or apple, rolled-up socks, bath toy)

1. **Thoroughly clean and rinse** the empty yoghurt pot and cut out the bottom of the pot with scissors. This creates the basketball hoop.

2. **Decorate the outside of the pot** with tape, hatching patterns, or with paint to create the appearance of a net.

3. **Once decorated,** secure the hoop to the wall or side of your bath with tape.

4. **Find a suitable basketball** – ours have ranged from bath toys or corks, to an apple – and get playing.

THE GARDEN, BALCONY
OR WINDOW

As a family, we love being outdoors – be it in the woods, the park or at the beach, come rain or shine. I feel so fortunate to have a spacious and secure garden, meaning I can open our back door and let the girls, and the dogs, roam free. Of course, life doesn't always lend itself to having a garden at all, and so I've created this chapter inspired by the garden. It should work for you whatever the size of your outdoor space, garden or not.

THE GREAT OUTDOORS

This section is for little ones who love the outdoors! From camping crafts and outdoor picnics to creating family favourite games with sticks and stones. It's all in here.

Cardboard campsite

Can't go camping yourselves? Then make a cardboard campsite! It's another much loved craft, simply made by folding strips of cardboard. It's one that Lily and Willow return to time and time again.

What you will need:
- 2 x cardboard sheets
- Ruler (or hardback book)
- Scissors (or craft knife, if you have one)
- Masking tape
- Glue
- Optional: scrap or tissue paper for details and decoration

FOR THE TENT

1. **Cut a rectangle** out of a cardboard sheet. Fold it into thirds, using a ruler or the spine of a book to achieve your straight line.

2. **Construct a pyramid shape** and use tape to secure.

3. **Cut a window** in each side of your tent by carving a 'cat flap' and fold it upwards to open.

4. **Add a square of tissue paper** to each tent for a duvet.

FOR THE SEATING AREA

1. **Cut another rectangle** out of the leftover cardboard sheet to make your communal table.

2. **Place it landscape in front of you.** Folding from left to right, fold a slim rectangle, then a wider rectangle, followed by another slim rectangle, then another large one. The slim rectangles and wider ones should be the same size to create a shallow cube. Trim any overhangs and tape to secure.

3. **To create the seats,** cut four more strips of cardboard, roll these into tubes and flatten. Add a tissue paper tablecloth and small cardboard plates to complete the dining experience!

FOR THE CAMP FIRE

1. **Cut two circles** of the same size from the cardboard. Cut out a smaller circle in the centre of one so it resembles a doughnut.

2. **Glue this doughnut** onto the larger circle. You can colour or paint the larger circle, if you want, before gluing down the doughnut. This base will represent the fire.

3. **Cut little strips of cardboard** for firewood. You can glue these down, although my girls enjoy carefully assembling and disassembling the campsite so our firewood is kept loose.

FOR THE SHOWER

1. **Cut a slim rectangle of cardboard** from the second sheet of cardboard and fold in half. Stand this upright as you would a greetings card.

2. **Cut out a shower head shape** from cardboard. We add lots of small pricks with a craft knife to create water holes.

3. **Next, cut a length of tape** and roll it into a tube to create your shower cord.

4. **Place this inside the card,** with the shower head on top and tape to secure.

5. **Finally, we added some tissue paper details:** a small shower mat and mirror on the opposite side to the shower.

FOR THE CAMPERVAN

1. **The campervan is made** in such a way that the roof can be lifted on and off to place play people inside.

2. **This is constructed in a similar way** to the tents but using two rectangles of cardboard.

3. **Fold each rectangle into thirds.** One is placed inverted on top of the other, as if making a box without sides. Trim the sides of the rectangle on top, so that the roof is more of a shallow lid.

4. **Cut four circles of cardboard** to create the wheels. Add masking tape in an asterisk shape to create the spokes of the wheel and glue them onto the sides of your campervan.

5. **A little like we did with the tent windows,** cut a sideways cat flap for a door. You could do the same on the roof for a skylight, too.

LITTER PICKING AT HOME

This is a 'taking care of the planet' play pursuit that helps reinforce the idea that our responsibility for the Earth is a shared one. This is a frequent go-to for the girls to play together. This activity allows you to practise through play in the home, setting an example for outdoor litter picking later on. Scatter clean recycling items around the house and get your little ones to collect up in a box or bag, using kitchen tongs. Depending on their age, you may choose to extend this by challenging them to sort the items by material once they are finished.

GARDEN PICNIC

As soon as the weather is warm enough, we eat most of our meals outside. Eating on the floor in picnic fashion is seen as much more exciting by the girls than eating at the table. Even on grey or rainy days, making our own garden picnic in the middle of the floor indoors, with a vase of flowers as a centrepiece sparks joy too. Set up your picnic, by bringing together suitable crockery from your house, a cosy blanket or sheet to sit on and any other extras that will put a smile on your and your little one's face.

CAMPING – INDOORS OR OUTDOORS

I've only very recently had my first camping trip with my children. It was high up on my bucket list but until our recent trip, the opportunity to go had not yet presented itself. So, my knowledge of camping mostly comes from my children's books, books I enjoyed when I was a girl and a jolly memory of working at a music festival as an Oxfam volunteer in my late teens. It was amazing to tick it off our bucket list at last. And until next time, we practise our camping pursuits indoors (or in fairer weather, in the garden). Here is our camping checklist.

What you will need:
- Tent (yours, or a children's one, or chairs and a big sheet)
- Sleeping bag (or blankets, towels, duvets, pillows etc.)
- Torch (or headlamp or candles)
- Snacks and containers (packed lunch boxes, flasks etc.)
- Optional: camping stories, games, wellington boots, warm clothes, first-aid kit, anything else you would like to take with you!)

THE TENT

The first order of duty is to prepare the campsite and this begins with the tent. Put up your own camping tent, if you have one and have enough space. Perhaps use the middle of the living room or the middle of your garden. A children's play tent would also work well for this. We have neither, so instead we gather dining chairs, arrange them in a circle with the seats facing outwards and throw a bedsheet on top for a fort-like tent.

SLEEPING BAGS, BLANKETS, PILLOWS

Gather whatever you have to add comfort to your campsite. Our go-to setup is a bed of towels, with sofa cushions in the middle and the girls' blankets thrown on top.

TORCH

This is a favoured piece of equipment here. We have a huge torch, which Lily loves playing with. Maybe you have a headtorch in your household, any torch will work, and if you can draw the curtains or dim the lights to add to the atmosphere, then even better.

SNACKS

Another little detail that really transforms the experience is how you consume your camping feast. Drinking out of flasks and eating from packed lunches adds to the magic.

ENTERTAINMENT

Gather camping stories to read in your campsite or take turns in making up your own stories.

EXTRAS

As much as the joy of camping is in the experience, setting up camp is equally part of the fun. Even if you don't end up using everything, it's a great learning opportunity to send your little ones hunting for other things you may need, such as welly boots, a warm hat or pots and pans.

Make your own slingshot

This craft made me very happy indeed. It took a few experiments but in the end, I found a robust way to make it, and here it is! The biggest fan of this one was Stuart. He was the first one to test it out, and getting it back from him was equally tricky work!

What you will need:
- Kitchen roll tube
- 2 x loo roll tubes
- A rubber band
- Scissors
- Tape
- Small scrap of cardboard (or whatever else you'd like to sling)

1. **Cut open the kitchen roll vertically** and then roll it into a tighter tube and tape to secure.

2. **Repeat this step** with the loo roll tubes to make two more slim tubes.

3. **Cut a small hole** in your kitchen roll tube just big enough for your loo tubes to sit in, at an angle, near the top.

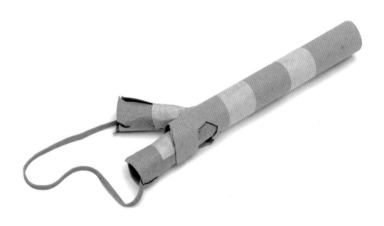

4. **When slotting the tubes in place** you may find that they don't fit together easily, given that they 'meet' inside the tube. I solved this by folding and squeezing in the ends of the tube to fit.

5. **Tape the loo roll tubes in place.** I needed quite a bit of tape to ensure it was robust enough for play with the kids.

6. **Trim the kitchen roll tube** between the loo roll tubes a little, so that whatever is slung doesn't get caught on this.

7. **Cut slits into the top of your loo roll tubes,** small enough to keep your band in place, and slide the rubber band through them, pulling it back towards you.

8. **Place a stone or scrap of cardboard** in your slingshot to sling.

STICKS AND STONES TIC TAC TOE

This is an ode to the family favourite, with a dose of nature thrown in. We keep pebbles in a jar on the kitchen worktop, ready to be taken outside to play this game on sunny days. If you don't have a stash of pebbles handy, then head outside to collect eight stones or pebbles. Divide these in half and paint in two different colours. If you don't have paint, you can mark half of them with a marker pen so as to differentiate between the two sets. Mark out a grid on the ground either using sticks, tape or cardboard strips. Divide the family into teams and get playing.

FLOWER ARRANGING

I adore flowers and trees (the girls' names may have
already given that away!) and in another life, I'd love
to have my own florist shop. I find it fascinating
watching the florists put bouquets together in my
local store. Better still, I love to watch Lily arranging
flowers with such focus and concentration. There are
lots of practical lessons that our children can take
from flower arranging. Naming parts of flowers,
practising using scissors while snipping stems, filling
up jugs or vases with water, carefully removing leaves
and so on. Lay flowers out on a plate or tray so that
they can be accessed easily. Let your little one fill up
a jug or vase with water. Explain the importance of
snipping the stems at an angle so that the flowers can
get a good drink and allow them to arrange them as
they choose.

Teddy bear swing

I made this swing from a box that Stuart's new bike helmet came in.
There was a tree in our garden that I wanted to hang a swing on for the
girls. I bought everything needed to make one except for the brackets to
secure the swing onto the tree! So, one Saturday morning, I had the idea
to craft the next best thing. This swing can be hung from a tree or in a
doorway of your house to be enjoyed come rain or shine.

What you will need:
- Shoebox
- Teddy bear (or two) of your child's choosing (teddies rather than dolls are better as they are light enough to swing)
- Scissors (and craft knife, if you have one)
- Twine
- Tape

1. **Remove the lid to the box** or any flaps that make a lid. Set these aside for use later.

2. **Place your teddy bears** into your box and ensure they're sitting comfortably.

3. **Using a craft knife,** or the blade of open scissors, cut out holes where the feet of the teddy bears sit. Once you've cut one hole, you can use the cut-out oval shape as a guide to cut the others.

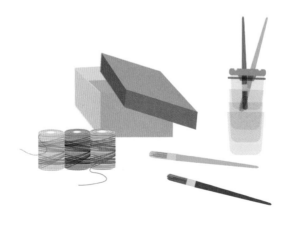

4. **Depending on the age of your teddy bears,** they may need straps. If so, you can use the shoebox lid to make these. Cut two long strips and roll, wriggle and bend them to make them more flexible and turn them into loops for armholes. This is a fun bit that your children can do.

5. **Tape the loops to the inside of the box,** sliding your teddy bear's arms into them.

6. **Now to create the hanging rope** for the swing: poke two holes in both sides of the swing. They need to be in the same position on both sides for balance.

7. **Cut four very long lengths of twine,** double the length of the height you are hanging your swing from. Feed one length through each hole – your helper could assist with this.

8. **If you're hanging your swing inside** in a doorway or on a fence, you can tie the lengths on each side together in a knot, leaving a little length at the end to tape to your doorway.

9. **If hanging your swing from a tree,** tie the lengths on each side together over a suitable branch.

BIRDS, FISH AND
OTHER CREATURES

I've used the following crafts to foster and grow my family's learning
of, and appreciation for, nature's many creatures. I've always found
spotting things in nature to be hugely uplifting, calming and very useful
for keeping me in the present. It's not something I've consciously passed
on to my children, in fact it may well be something they've thought to do
of their own accord in the way that little ones so often do. Either way, I
love that it's our thing to do together. Noticing the green of the leaves,
finding flowers in the dirt, following butterflies and ladybugs or listening
to the hum of bees.

There are bugs that the girls love, others they strongly dislike, but they
find birds magical and are fascinated by fish. Of all of these creatures,
they ask a hundred and one questions, and in looking up answers for
them, I've learned a lot myself – from what store-cupboard items are
optimal for feeding birds, to why ladybugs have spots.

Fishing game

I made this craft for Lily in our first house in France. She enjoyed painting her fish first, before catching them all with her rod. Every so often we add more fish to our swarm, this being yet another craft we return to often.

What you will need:
- Cardboard sheet
- 1 x kitchen roll tube
- 1 x loo roll tube
- Tape

1. **Begin by cutting out plenty of sea creature shapes** from the cardboard sheet – our favourites are fish, crabs and lobsters. Once cut, decorate the shapes.

2. **Cut the loo roll tube** into horizontal strips – enough for each of your sea creatures, with one extra.

3. **Tape a cardboard strip into place in a loop shape** on the back of each of your sea creatures (A).

4. **To create the fishing rod,** cut the kitchen roll in half vertically. Roll it into a tighter tube and tape into place.

5. **Cut the remaining loo roll strip** in half and then wrap it around your finger to achieve a semi-circle shape. Place this inside the top of your cardboard rod and tape to secure and create the hook (B).

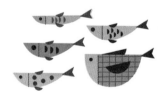

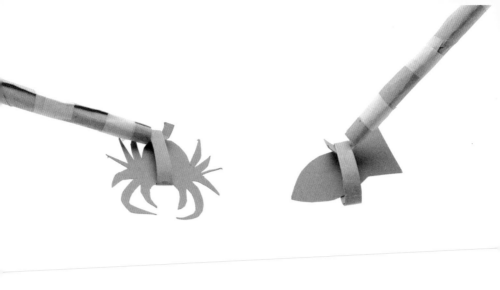

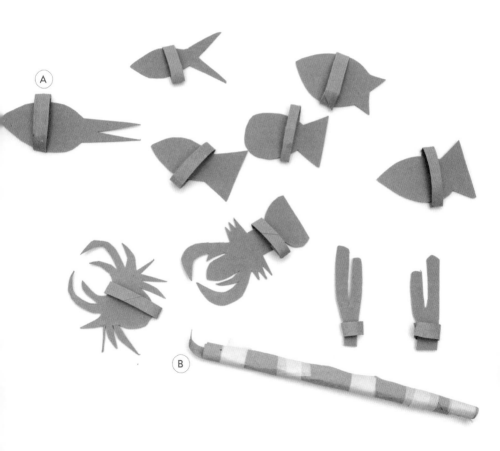

— 179 —

Tin-can bug hotel

There's a repetitive rhythm to this craft, which is perfect for grown-ups and children who enjoy that. Essentially, all you need to do is fill a tin can with rolled up loo roll tubes, which make wonderful burrows for insects to dwell in. You'll need quite a few tubes – we used eleven loo rolls the last time we made this!

What you will need:
- A tin can
- Multiple loo roll tubes (or kitchen roll tubes, if using a larger can)
- Scissors
- Tape
- Optional: pencil, sticks, leaves, twine

1. **Rinse and clean a tin can** and check it for a sharp rim. To ensure we don't cut ourselves, I usually fold a length of tape around the top of the can.

2. **Cut the loo roll tubes in half** vertically and then in half again. Create two new thinner tubes by rolling these around a pencil, before taping into place – this is a nice job for independent crafters to do themselves.

3. **Once your two new slimmer tubes are rolled,** place these inside your tin can. You may need to trim the ends of the tubes slightly depending on the size of the can. You want the tubes to hang over the edge of the can a little.

4. **Repeat this sequence** until your tin is full of tubes that fit snugly without being squashed and do not fall out when the can is turned upside down.

5. **Once you are happy** with your bug hotel, you can either leave the can outside at ground level or tie a length of twine around it so that you can hang it up outside.

6. **Be mindful of where** you are leaving it. If leaving it outside of your own garden, take note of 'litter laws' in public spaces.

'THROUGH THE LOOKING GLASS'
BUG STUDY

Whether your young ones love creepy crawlies or
need some encouragement to engage with them
closely (I have one of each), we find this is a great
way to explore and appreciate insects close up. Cut a
circle out of the top curved part of a large plastic
bottle. This circular shallow bowl when filled with a
few drops of water becomes a magnifying glass! Go
on the hunt for creepy crawlies in dark corners of the
house or secluded areas of the garden, taking your
makeshift glass and a small cup of water with you.
Notice and observe creatures, pointing out wings,
colours, number of legs and so on. Be careful not to
spill your water and get your creatures wet!

Bird watching and feeding

This is a project that both of my older girls can enjoy together. As Willow is nineteen months younger than Lily, there are often things she has been too young to join in with initially. Luckily, at the time I first made this for the girls, Willow was able to join in straightaway, decanting seeds into the bird feeders and shouting happily as she spotted birds that came to visit. I first made this in autumn and so playing with it was more of an opportunity to talk about birds rather than see them. When we returned to it in the spring, it was amazing! It invited so many birds into the garden the girls were delighted and it shot up on their list of favourite cardboard toys.

What you will need:
- Cardboard box
- 2 x loo roll tubes
- Egg carton
- Scissors (and craft knife, if you have one)
- Tape and glue
- Optional: tissue paper, ruler, twine, bird food (bread or toast crumbs, seeds and even cooked rice work very well)

FOR THE BIRD HOUSE

1. **Begin by creating the pointed roof line of a house.** Remove a right-angled triangle from each corner of the top of the cardboard box. You can cut these off carefully with scissors or a craft knife.

2. **Next, add a peep hole for the birds.** I use one of the loo roll tubes as a guide for this. Place it in position and trace around it lightly with the blade of your scissors or craft knife before cutting it out completely.

3. **Through the open roof of the box,** you can add shredded cardboard or tissue paper at the bottom of the box.

4. **From the scraps you cut to create your pointed roof,** cut one wide strip of cardboard and fold it in half. Position this above the uncovered roof space of your bird house and tape into place to create your roof.

5. **If you have some twine,** tape a length of it to the back of the house so it can be hung from a fence or tree outside.

FOR THE BIRD BOWLS

1. **Take an egg carton** and cut out pairs of cups. Cut close to the bowl shape that the cartons naturally make.

2. **Cut a length of twine** and tie it together in a knot around the bridge of your bowls. Leave the twine lengths long so as you can hang them up in your garden.

FOR THE BINOCULARS

These are a loo roll craft classic and as such there are a great many variations to making these. We make these as follows but if you have your own preferred method already, then use that for your kit!

1. **Cut both loo roll tubes open vertically,** roll them in tighter to create slightly smaller tubes then tape into place.

2. **Cut a cardboard strip** from scraps of cardboard left over and use this to connect your rolls together.

3. **Attach a long length of twine** to the cardboard centrepiece of your binoculars so that it can be worn around your little one's neck. Do be careful, of course, with anything you tie around the neck of your child.

MAKING SEASONAL DISPLAYS

Bring the outside in and connect with nature through this mindful activity. Lily and Willow are forever filling my pockets on walks or running inside from the garden with collections of seasonal treasures. Conkers in autumn, wildflowers in spring – we seem to have a never-ending mountain of forages. It has become a fun and therapeutic task to make an arrangement from these items on a dish, which then sits on the kitchen table or cabinet and can be altered as the seasons change. Wilted bits are removed, newly found pieces are added, and sometimes we embark on an entire overhaul. There are so many opportunities for learning and exploration through this simple task – comments to be made about the colours of the various treasures, their smell, if any, how delicate, rough or smooth they are. You can extend your nature arranging further, by drawing your treasures. For very young ones, just offering colours that match the display is enough to get them started.

TIME OF DAY AND SEASONS

I remember as a child returning to school in the autumn, reuniting with friends after the long summer holiday and at harvest festival loudly singing 'Autumn Days' in the school hall. Winter, I love now for its dark afternoons, which are gloriously cosy once you're at home, the promise of Christmas and of new year's resolutions. Spring brings magnolia, frogspawn and the clocks going forward. While summer brings my birthday, a season for packing picnics and packing suitcases. As I've got older I've become quite ritualistic, loving the creations and traditions adopted with each passing season and taking delight in sharing these with the girls.

Telescope

Like the cardboard camera (see page 94), this is a perfect craft for young artists to make completely independently. This is a project that I suggest when the girls and I want to craft different things, but side by side. I give them a tube each to decorate and I craft my own thing next to them.

What you will need:
- Kitchen roll tube
- Colouring pencils or paint, or scrap paper and glue
- Optional: scissors, tape

1. **Make the kitchen roll tube** into a thinner tube by cutting it open vertically, rolling it in slightly and then taping back into position.

2. **Alternatively,** you can simply leave the kitchen roll tube as is, and decorate it as you wish.

Stargazing

Lily absolutely loves the moon. The brilliant sunshine and mostly cloud-free days that we enjoy in France mean we often have perfect skies for moon watching in the evenings, and it's something we enjoy doing as a family. For fellow young astronomers, stargazing is a wonderful activity. Go outdoors on a clear night and take in the moon and stars. Lay a blanket down on the ground and lie down to face the night sky. If you have binoculars, you can take these with you, but they're not essential for stargazing. We never use them, but on occasion have used a homemade telescope (see above) as a fun prop.

Watching the sunrise and sunset

One of my favourite ways to start or end the day is to watch the sun
come up or go down. So much so that I've been known to set my alarm
for 4.30am to watch it from my spare bedroom window (the best view in
the house). Depending on timings in your house, your children may not
be able to enjoy the sun's comings and goings with you, but there are so
many ways to enjoy them in your own time. Watch the sunrise or sunset
together from a garden or window, if you can, or draw the sunrise or
sunset together. Drawing together is a lovely way to connect. Afterwards,
stick the picture up in the window using tape, so you can watch a sunrise
or sunset that is your very own. Sometimes, we gather stories that
reference the sun coming up or going down and read them together
back to back. We look at the photos and point out colours, any animals
and what people are doing. This is an especially calm way to spend some
time in the early morning or when winding down at night.

HOW DOES YOUR GARDEN GROW?

While I'm no budding horticulturist, I do find such satisfaction and calm from my amateur green-fingered pursuits. I've really enjoyed trying things for the first time with the girls and also sharing with them the joy of crafting with, or inspired by, nature.

Gardening tools

Willow loves the sensory exploration of being out in the garden so much that I was keen to create some gardening tools for her to play with indoors on wet or windy days. This is how this gardening tools set came about.

What you will need:
- 4 x loo roll tubes (2 per tool)
- Cardboard sheet
- Scissors
- Tape

1. **Cut two loo roll tubes in half vertically,** then roll each into a tighter tube and tape to secure. These become the handles to your tools.

2. **For the trowel,** take a third loo roll tube and cut an oval scooped shape opening out of it.

3. **For the fork,** take a fourth loo roll tube and cut three prong shapes at one end.

4. **Now to put your tools together.** Cut thin strips from a cardboard sheet and tape these around the handles. Keep adding until you can slot this handle into the head of your tool without much movement. You can tape to further secure, if you need to.

DON'T THROW IT, GROW IT!

From seed to sprout

Gardening is something I'd love to get more involved with. I have romantic ideas of a future me going into my back garden with a basket and pulling up vegetables that I then prepare for dinner. It's somewhat blown my mind to learn that you can actually begin growing vegetables from vegetable scraps. Of course, to grow them fully, you eventually need soil, appropriate weather conditions and patience – avocados can take five years to yield fruit. Yet engaging in the early process in this way is a great way for little ones to witness the stages that usually take place below ground, while learning about growth and gardening in the process.

What you will need:
- Food scraps (lettuce leaf, celery base, avocado seed)
- Three toothpicks (for avocado)
- Glass (for avocado)
- Spray bottle (for leafy veg)
- Dish (for other food scraps)
- Water

LETTUCE

For lettuce, place leftover leaves in a bowl with a bit of water at the bottom. Place the bowl in a spot that gets good sunlight and spray the leaves with water a few times each week. After four or so days you should see roots and new leaves appear. Now you can transfer your leaves into soil.

CELERY

Place the base of the celery in a bowl with a little warm water at the bottom. Keep the bowl in direct sunlight. After a week the leaves begin to thicken. Once this happens you can transfer your celery into soil.

AVOCADO

You can use an entire avocado with this book, eating the flesh on toast, using the skin for boats (see page 149) and growing a new tree from the seed! Wash the seed and establish which is the top and bottom. Pierce the bottom of the seed with three toothpicks and suspend over water in a bowl or glass. The water should cover the bottom of the seed. Keep the container in a warm spot but avoiding direct sunlight. This one requires patience as it can take up to six weeks for the stem and roots to appear. Check your seed with your child each day, adding water as needed. Once roots appear, you'll need to trim them a little until you see leaves. Once you have leaves you can plant the seed in soil.

Tin-can flowerpots

Repurposing empty tin cans into flowerpots is so easily done and is a simple way to demonstrate the many possibilities of re-use in the home. Tin-can flowerpots also make great gifts, either empty or with a fresh pot of herbs inside! Begin by washing out any empty tin cans completely, taking care with the rim in case there are any sharp edges. An optional step is to drill or pierce holes at the bottom of your tin to allow for drainage (don't worry if you don't do this, just sit plants inside in their own drainage pot). Paint or cover the labels in collage to decorate. Add soil, along with herbs or a flower.

Vegetable garden

This is a lovely craft to promote discussion about vegetables with your children and perhaps to encourage trying lesser known or lesser preferred ones! You can play with this in a number of different ways, from planting vegetables of the same colour or planting vegetables by name, to the many ways your children will invent themselves.

What you will need:
- Egg carton
- Cardboard sheet
- Loo roll tubes (1 loo roll makes 4 vegetables)
- Scissors
- Tape
- Pen or pencil

1. **Turn the egg carton upside down** and pierce a hole in each compartment with scissors.

2. **Open this up to create a larger hole** with your finger. This acts as your vegetable bed.

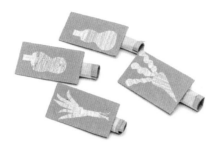

3. **Cut small rectangles out of the cardboard sheet** that are no wider than each carton compartment and a little taller.

4. **On these rectangles,** draw your chosen vegetables, which your little ones can colour in.

5. **Cut the loo roll tubes into quarters** vertically. Roll each one up tightly to form smaller tubes that will fit inside the egg carton holes. Tape these together to secure.

6. **Tape these thinner tubes** to the back of each vegetable rectangle, so that you can plant your cards into your vegetable bed.

MAKE YOUR OWN SOIL

To create your own soil to use with your gardening set, you can blitz or bash any stale, brown foods (bran, brown cereal or brown biscuits work well). Throw this into a box or baking tray to be used with gardening tools (see page 193). This is a great sensory activity, that is also taste-safe for very young children.

FLOWER PRESSING

Pressing flowers is the perfect way to treasure blooms that have sparked joy. Flowers received on birthdays or picked by our neighbour's little boy for the girls or found on family walks, have all been pressed by us and enjoyed once again later on. For children, this is a good exercise in patience, something that features a lot in gardening. The wait is worth it when the results are discovered weeks later. You can use pressed flowers for pictures, to decorate glassware (applying a coat of water-based glue to stick them and another coat of glue afterwards), or for thank you cards (see page 74). Flowers are best pressed before they begin to wilt. Wildflowers, such as daisies and poppies, look amazing when pressed. Lay your chosen flowers on a sheet of baking paper and place between two sheets of cardboard before stacking a pile of heavy books on top. Leave for a fortnight or two. Use tweezers to lift the pressed flowers carefully from their baking paper sandwich. Using thin strips of tape to secure pressed stems onto a card is a simple elegant touch, or try water-based glue, if you prefer.

LOO ROLL VEHICLES

While cardboard comes and goes in our house, depending on cereal consumption, recent deliveries and our latest crafting pursuits, we seem to forever have an abundance of toilet roll tubes. They're undoubtedly far easier to come by and so, for a while, I concentrated my efforts on crafting with them as much as possible and before long I found myself with a collection of vehicles. As they are constructed from loo roll tubes, the vehicles are all quite small, but I like that about them. They're perfect for little hands to travel with around the room. That said, you'll need pretty tiny passengers to fit inside (the passengers, of course, are not essential). Alternatively, you can use the loo roll finger puppets from this book (see page 121). These vehicles journey higher in the sky with the more loo roll tubes you use, with four loo roll tubes taking you all the way to outer space!

Car

The entirety of the car can be made only with loo rolls, if you are careful to set aside the scraps. However, if you prefer a car that sports larger than life wheels, these can be created with spare bottle caps or even just cut out from scrap cardboard.

What you will need:
- 1 x loo roll tube
- Scissors
- Tape or glue
- Optional: 4 bottle caps or a scrap of cardboard for extra-large wheels

1. **Fold a loo roll tube** in half and flatten it.

2. **Cut a small semi-circle** in the middle of the longer side, then reopen the tube. This opening is where the driver will sit.

3. **Cut four small circles** from the discarded circle you have cut. These will become the wheels. Your little one may want to decorate these before you glue to each corner of the car.

4. **If you find these wheels too small,** you can cut larger ones from scrap cardboard, paper or find bottle caps to use instead.

RAILWAY CHILDREN WATCHING

The Railway Children by Edith Nesbit was a childhood favourite of mine. For those who don't know it, it's about three siblings, Bobby, Peter and Phyllis, who entertain themselves by watching the trains on the nearby railway line and waving to the passengers. Remembering this inspired me to think up a game where Lily and I could spot and wave at vehicles ourselves. This worked perfectly when we lived in London, living on a fairly busy road where there was an abundance of vehicles for us to wave at from a window. I scribbled tally charts for red cars, blue cars, police cars and so on, and we would spot and count them. In rural France, living off the beaten track, there are far fewer cars to spot. So, we lie on our backs in the garden and spot planes instead, or we choose storybooks and make our tally charts through looking at the pictures.

Hot air balloon

This cardboard vehicle also makes a cute mobile.

What you will need:
- 2 x loo roll tubes
- Scissors
- Tape
- String or twine

1. **Take the first loo roll tube** and cut vertical slits from the bottom almost to the top all the way around the tube. I cut eight around mine.

2. **Roll each strip inwards** around your finger so that they create a globe. Secure in place with tape and you have your balloon.

3. **Next, take a second loo roll tube** and cut four slits (in the north, east, south and west positions) from the bottom of the tube to halfway up the tube.

4. **Fold these slits into the tube** so as to create a flat base. Trim the top flap a little so that you can tape into place. This creates your basket.

5. **Tape two identical lengths** of twine onto both the balloon and basket to connect them.

6. **Finally, thread a longer length of twine** through the top of your balloon so you can hang, carry or fly it.

Aeroplane

Three empty loo rolls makes a wonderfully detailed plane with lots of space for your little ones to add designs and decorations. Our planes are played with endlessly.

What you will need:
- 3 x loo roll tubes
- Scissors
- Tape

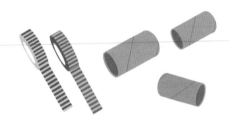

1. **Cut open a loo roll tube vertically.** Open up and flatten. From this, cut out a piece in the shape of a plane's silhouette.

2. **Next, take a second loo roll tube** and fold in half and flatten. Cut a small semi-circle in the middle of the longer side, then reopen.

3. **Place this second tube on top** of your cut-out plane shape and glue or tape in place.

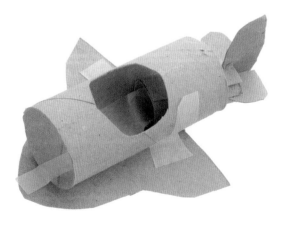

4. **Take a third loo roll tube** and cut in half horizontally.

5. **Take one half and cut in half vertically.** Roll it in tighter to create a narrower tube shape and tape to secure.

6. **Make four slits** in this narrower tube, as if cutting at the north, east, south and west positions on a compass.

7. **Take the other half** of the third loo roll tube and cut in half vertically. Open and flatten. Cut out two oval shapes.

8. **Slot one oval** into the west-east slit in your narrow tube. Cut a slit in the middle of this oval.

9. **Slide your remaining oval** into your north-south slit and through the slit of the oval just cut. This is your plane's rudder. Tape or glue this to the inside of your tube.

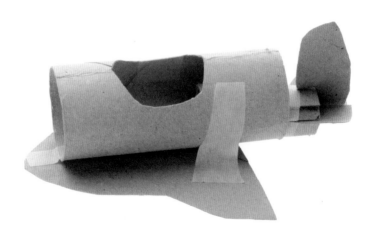

Rocket ship

What you will need:
- 4 x loo roll tubes
- Scissors
- Tape and or glue

1. **Cut open the first loo roll tube** vertically. Cut vertical lines close together from the bottom almost to the top.

2. **Roll these strips up vertically** to varying lengths. Then roll the whole tube back together and tape in place. This will be the fire for your rocket ship and can be decorated, if you like (A).

3. **Flatten the second loo roll** and cut a small semi-circle in the middle of the long side. Reopen the tube. This is the window (B).

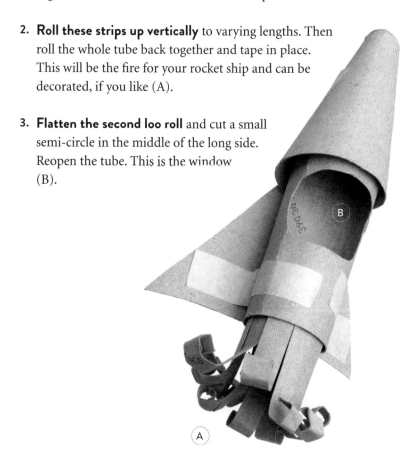

4. **Slot the fire tube** into the base of the window tube.

5. **Cut open a third loo roll tube** vertically and flatten.

6. **From this, cut a triangle shape** and tape this to the back of your window tube (C).

7. **Cut open the final tube vertically.** Construct a cone shape and tape into place to secure.

8. **Place this cone on top** of your window tube (D).

9. **If you want to put a play person inside** this rocket, place two strips of tape across the fire tube of your rocket for them to sit on. You can then remove and replace the cone head of your rocket to be able to move them in and out!

I do so hope you have enjoyed the crafts and games within this book and that you go on to use them over and over again with your children. Creating a book which incorporates so much of what is important to me – family connection, slower paced living and care for the environment has been such a wonderful opportunity. As our global awareness and understanding for the importance of sustainability and environmentalism grows, my hope is that this book becomes a valuable tool in making a difference in the world of play.

FURTHER READING AND RESOURCES

I've found the following to be invaluable resources in my day to day parenting. This list is not exhaustive, but these are the books, websites and Instagram accounts I find myself referencing time and time again.

Food and Cooking

One pan style cooking has been quite the gamechanger for our family:

Anna Jones, *One Pot, Pan, Planet: A Greener Way to Cook for You and Your Family and the Planet*, Fourth Estate, 2021

Rachel Ama, *One Pot: Three Ways*, Yellow Kite, 2021

Our family's favourite recipe book for all things sweet:

Ravneet Gill, *The Pastry Chef's Guide: The Secret to Successful Baking Every Time*, Pavilion Books, 2020 (especially for the cookie recipe on page 103!)

For weaning and food ideas for young ones (that all the family can enjoy) we love:

Boob to food, www.boobtofood.com, and find her on Instagram @boobtofood

Mama eats plants, www.mamaeatsplants.com, and find her on Instagram @mamaeatsplants

The girls' favourite children's recipe books to cook from are:

Adina Chitu, *Tasty Treats: Easy Cooking for Children*, Little Gestalten, 2020

Felicity Sala, Lunch at 10 Pomegranate Street, Scribble UK, 2019

For all things fun with food, birthday cake and party food ideas, all super doable, see my wonderful friend Rachel at Sweet and Savage, www.sweetandsavage.co.nz

Motherhood

I've found great comfort, resonance and understanding in the words of fellow mothers.

The following are among some of my favourites books.

Clover Stroud, *My Wild and Sleepless Nights: A Mother's Story*, Doubleday, 2020

Candice Brathwaite, *I Am Not Your Baby Mother*, Quercus, 2020

Hollie McNish, *Nobody Told Me*, Fleet, 2020

Approaches to Parenting

I have taken so much from the following parenting pages, podcasts and books.

Simone Davies, *The Montessori Toddler*, Workman Publishing, 2019

Heng Ou with Amely Greeven and Marisa Belger, *The First Forty Days: The Essential Art of Nourishing the New Mother*, Stewart, Tabori & Chang, 2016

Hollie de Cruz, *Your Baby, Your Birth,* Vermilion, 2018

Hollie de Cruz, *Motherhood Your Way*, Vermilion, 2021

The Good Enough Parent, The School of Life Press, 2021

We Nurture Collective podcast and on Instagram @we_nurture

Whole Beings on Instagram @ whole.beings

Curious Parenting on Instagram @ curious.parenting

Children's Books

Our family has far too many favourites to list all of them!

One of our all-time favourite authors is Trish Cooke

We love picture books by Little Gestalten

And poetry for children: William Sieghart, *Everyone Sang: A Poem for Every Feeling*, Walker Books, 2021

Eco Living, Home and the Outdoors

Christine Liu, *Sustainable Home*, White Lion Publishing, 2018

Aja Barber, *Consumed: The Need for Collective Change*, Octopus, 2021

Poppy Okotcha, www.poppyokotcha.com, or follow her on Instagram @poppyokotcha

The Sustainable Camping Company on Instagram @thesustainablecampingco

Seek by iNaturalist, the app for identifying plants and animals

We have found an abundance of nature-inspired projects to try on www.woodlarkblog

Mindfulness and Joy

These are the books I reach for to find joy, or in moments of joy.

William Sieghart, *The Poetry Pharmacy*, Particular Books, 2017

Yung Pueblo, *Clarity & Connection*, Andrews McMeel Publishing, 2021

Small Pleasures, The School of Life Press, 2016

Cleo Wade, *Heart Talk*, Atria Books, 2018

Cleo Wade, *Where to Begin*, Atria Books, 2020

INDEX

ACKNOWLEDGEMENTS

There are so many wonderful people who have supported and inspired me, not only in the journey to this book, but my motherhood journey too.

Jane. My straight-talking and very kind agent. Thank you for your belief in me, your encouragement and for gently guiding me through this process.

The team at Greenfinch and Quercus. Kerry, Nicole, Julia, Tokiko, Pui and Michael. Thank you for your wonderful designs, ideas, illustrations, photos, patience (!) and for bringing *Sustainable Play* to life.

In the early days when this book lived only in my mind, there were some incredible women who showed me such generosity in their time, their sharing of my work, and their championing of me.

Grace. From your offer of a zoom call to a practical stranger, to countless messages of advice and encouragement, I am so, so grateful to you for your unending support and friendship.

Clover. You are hugely inspirational, wonderfully supportive and unwaveringly kind.

Mary. Magic Mary – you are always so supportive, so enthusiastic, and bring such sparkly, positive energy.

Laura. Thank you for your friendship, your creative inspiration, the longest, most glorious WhatsApp voice notes, and all the joy you bring.

Daisy. I speak for a great many parents worldwide, you have given us far more than five minutes! You consistently support, share endless ideas, and show so much kindness.

Lauren. Thank you thank you thank you. For championing and connecting me with Jane, for your mentorship, your advice, and your ears!

Before book writing, and after many years of following and reading, I was invited to contribute to Babyccino, the longstanding parenting blog where I made lifelong friends.

Esther. Thank you for welcoming me with open arms, not only into your business but into your home.

Zainab. Here's to a lot more laughter, to more 'behind the scenes', and to that special understanding of each other that comes from a great many shared experiences.

Courtney, how wonderful it has been to connect with you, from the other side of the world! Thank you for your words and your wisdom.

This book was also made possible by communities.

To my glorious Instagram community. Modern day tech and social media often gets a bad rep (often by me), but I am so, so thankful to have connected with so many fellow crafters, parents, and people. To all those that have liked, followed, messaged, saved and shared. A huge, huge thank you.

Village Books. I couldn't mention community without including you! The bookshop I grew up in, where not only did my love of books grow, but my dream to write one. Thank you Tracy and Hazel, for creating such a special haven.

This book was written while pregnant with my third daughter and during my family's first year in France. To say it was a busy time would be a huge understatement and it would not have been achievable without some very special people.

Charlie, Jack, Miri and Luke. What a team you four are. Our first days in France were spent with you, where you happily trialled so many *Sustainable Play* games. Thank you for your enthusiasm, for our Thursday afternoons and for being such incredible friends.

Maria. Thank you for the loving, creative energy you have brought to our girls, our lives and our home. And for the great many craft ideas! Enough to fill another book!

Prunelle. They say it takes a village to raise a child, you have been our village in France. Thank you for all the time, support, and love you have shown our family. I could not have put pen to paper without you. Je t'aime trop.

Back home in London, live some of the greatest women ever!

Leila, Isabel, Sabrina, Sophie, Hannah. The best ever girl tribe. Thank you for being by my side for so many moments, big and small. Whilst having children first has at felt times felt lonely, you girls have reminded me I am never alone. You embrace my children just as you embrace me and are such epic, incredible women.

Rachel. What a sensation you are. Creative, inspiring, hilarious, fun. Not every day you are waiting for an iron transfusion in hospital and meet a fellow pregnant woman across the ward sporting pink fairy lights around her bed! Ever grateful for that day. Thank you for your friendship, your fun and for always being up for gin and a chat.

Alice. Thank you for all the fun, love,

and creativity you showed Lily, and a very tiny Willow! We dreamed of this book together! Thank you for believing that the dream would come true.

Harriet. Whether near or far, you will always be "wifey", thank you for being just who you are. With me, with the girls, you are magnificent.

Emma. Where would I be without you!? I do not know. I can tell you anything and everything (and I do), I can laugh with you, I can cry with you. You make each member of our family feel so loved. You are always been such a loyal and loving friend – ever since we were kids. You are one seriously special soul and I love you.

Syd. 24 years of friendship and counting. My best friend, my twin. How lucky I am to have thoughtful, loving, beautiful you. Oh how I love you. Here's to the next 24 and beyond.

And now to my family. This book would not exist without them. Nor would this version of me.

Stuart. My darling husband, my bestest friend, my Sp, my co-conspirator in all things 'making dreams come true'. I love that my life is with you. We have shared the most epic adventures, made the most amazing children, and created such a beautiful life together. Thank you for all that you do for me, for our girls, for us, and for dancing with me, always. ILYTTMABADATBH.

And to my three darling girls. All for you. Put simply each of you are pure magic and beyond my wildest dreams. Thank you for choosing for me. I love you more than I could ever put into words. I am having the time of my life being your Mum.

First published in Great Britain in 2022 by

Greenfinch
An imprint of Quercus Editions Ltd
Carmelite House
50 Victoria Embankment
London EC4Y 0DZ

An Hachette UK company

A CIP catalogue record for this book is available from the British Library

PB ISBN 978-1-52941-664-0
ebook ISBN 978-1-52941-665-7

10 9 8 7 6 5 4 3 2 1

Design by Tokiko Morishima
Illustrations by Pui Lee

Printed in China

Papers used by Greenfinch are from well-managed forests and other
responsible sources.